Construction Marketing Ideas

**Practical strategies and resources to attract
and retain profitable clients for your architectural,
engineering or construction business**

Mark Buckshon

Asset Beam Publishing Ltd.
Ottawa, Canada

ISBN 0-9810816-01
For additonal information, visit
http://www.constructionmarketingideas.com

Acknowledgements

Years ago, I discovered I could write quickly and innovatively, though the learning process did not occur instantly: I struggled as patient editors at *The Ubyssey*, the student newspaper at the University of British Columbia in Vancouver, showed me the basics of the inverted pyramid and journalistic writing.

These skills have served me well through my lifetime, as I graduated from journalism to public relations and finally, entrepreneurship, and my career as a publisher.

However, one goal has remained elusive: Writing a full-scale and comprehensive book. It is one thing to put together a brief news story, or even a thoroughly researched magazine article, but it is quite another to write hundreds of pages over months of time and research.

Writing coach Cindy Shearer helped me get started in framing my thoughts. I also received invaluable guidance from friends I have connected with through the Society for Marketing Professional Services (SMPS), including Tim Klabunde, Matt Handal, Mel Lester and Ford Harding, along with SMPS Marketer editor Randy Pollock.

As well, several people have contributed worthy insights and suggestions through the *Construction Marketing Ideas* blog including the late Sonny Lykos, and Leonard Megliola, and several regular contributors to the Remodel Crazy and Contractor Talk forums. Designer Raymond Levielle helped shape the book into the form you are reading.

My biggest debt of gratitude, however, is to my wife Vivian. She braved her way through early drafts, pointing out glaring weaknesses in the writing and suggested major changes. However, in the end, she asked me to take responsibility for my own writing, so what you are seeing here is my work; it will be mine to correct.

Since my business, after all, is publishing, I decided to publish this book under the imprint of one of the Construction News and Report Group of Companies, using Lightning Source (www.lightningsource.com) as the printer.

Using print-on-demand technologies, we can also update the book and correct errors quickly for subsequent editions. If you see anything in these pages you think needs to be changed, please email me at buckshon@cnrgp.com.

Ottawa, Ontario, January 1, 2010.

Table of contents

Part I
Foundations for effective architectural, engineering and construction industry marketing

Part II
Practical marketing observations and suggestions

Conclusion

Appendixes

Construction Marketing Ideas

**Practical strategies and resources to attract
and retain profitable clients for your architectural,
engineering or construction business**

PART I

Foundations for effective architectural, engineering and construction industry marketing

Chapter 1

Discover the secrets to successful construction marketing in both good and hard times

Every day, in good times and hard, your architectural, engineering or construction business encounters a fundamental challenge: How can you serve enough of the right clients, effectively, to ensure your profitability and success?

Your response, "Market your business wisely," takes you down two paths. You could say "I agree, but how?" If you are less familiar with marketing, you may simply ask: "Why?"

You are responding correctly either way.

Regardless of your answer, you can achieve construction marketing success with some simple changes in the way you conduct your business. These improvements won't cost you much money, if any, and you'll enjoy your business more. The secret to marketing success is effective branding, and this success comes from providing great service to your current clients and doing what you enjoy. In other words, you will have fun.

You don't need to be a great marketer to succeed in marketing construction services

You don't need to be great at marketing to achieve truly impressive results. Construction industry marketing is a new discipline. The primary association dedicated to architectural, engineering and construction (AEC) marketing, The Society for Marketing Professional Services (SMPS), is less than four decades old, born in 1973 at an American Institute of Architects conference. (The association now has more than 6,500 members with chapters in most major U.S. cities and in Toronto, Canada.)

The newness of marketing for the construction community means that competitive barriers to entry and success are not as great as for most other industries, which have amassed many years of expertise and research. In fact, you simply need to adapt some techniques long proven elsewhere to your business or career, and you will both succeed and stand out from the crowd. In the construction industry, a little marketing knowledge will take you a long way. This book will give you the insights you need to succeed, and warn you of a few pitfalls and dangers along the way.

What branding is, and why it is important

Few contractors, engineers or architects think about branding. Branding for most of us is an arcane concept, more appropriate to consumer products like Coca-Cola, or big businesses with huge advertising budgets like American Express. When you think about branding, you might also be thinking: "Will spending time on getting my business logo right really do me any good, and does advertising actually work in this industry?" and you are right to be skeptical. You will see that effective branding for your construction business has little to with your logos or advertising campaigns. It has everything to do with how you connect, serve and relate to your clients.

With great branding, you will overcome "lower price" competition

When you understand branding, you will earn higher margins than your competition; you won't fight endless, futile battles for "low bid wins the job" projects; and each morning, you will wake up looking forward to your day's work.

To give a personal example, I have been publishing regional newspapers and websites for the AEC industry for more than 15 years, and only learned how branding really works when the late Sonny Lykos, just months before his death in 2007, responded with some comments to my *Construction Marketing Ideas* blog. Lykos spent his lifetime building construction businesses before "semi-retiring" in Naples, Florida. (He probably worked harder than most people with regular jobs in his later years, combining a condominium maintenance business with incredible hours of voluntary communication with other contractors and providing advice on business and marketing concerns.)

Sonny sent me a package of materials, referred me to some excellent books, and explained that the secret to marketing success in this industry is almost entirely related to the branding experience you create for your clients and employees.

Branding is your entire client experience process

"Branding is simply what the customer(s) thinks of you," Lykos wrote. "It's that simple. It's not a logo. It's not a discount. It's not 'only' the calibre of your work. Their perception is based upon a compilation of every single contact anyone from your company has had with them . . . ."

Your first and most important construction marketing priority is ensuring your brand is right. This means getting your entire client experience process – including the relationships between clients and your employees – to the point where your clients perceive your business as resonating with their values, interests, and requirements. These perceptions of course will vary, depending on whether your clients are high-end executives, middle-class homeowners, or government agency project managers.

Of course, your clients don't want to be treated in a cookie-cutter, one-size-fits-all fashion. Nevertheless, they are almost all seeking consistency and reliability in your work. Clients have certain expectations which you can capture and respect in your marketing strategies. Your branding objective is to ensure your clients truly enjoy their experience, and truly feel that they've been served well.

You can achieve these successes with some simple process improvements, such as how you handle and return phone calls, your daily job site clean-up policies, and your response to any client worries or concerns. You can and should measure your success at these initiatives, but you need to go beyond the obvious, to your own passion and interests, to communicate shared values.

Focus on your passions, interests and pleasures. Your clients will appreciate your enthusiasm.

While you must remember your need to earn a profit, I believe that to succeed at construction industry marketing you must shift your focus from your business needs to your passions, interests, and pleasures, and relate these values to your current and potential clients.

For example, Sonny Lykos, based in Naples, Florida, appeared to have nothing to gain from communicating with me. I don't operate or manage a condominium in southwestern Florida needing maintenance services (his business) and could not refer any clients to him. But that wasn't the point. Sonny connected. He appreciated my knowledge about construction marketing issues, and simply wanted to share his own interest in the topic. He respected something I will elaborate on later in this book. If you do what you enjoy, and freely share your passions, you will achieve surprising and effective marketing results, regardless of whether or not you reap any immediate gain from your initiatives.

In his emails and letters, Sonny explained how he found clients willing to pay his price – and virtually never would this price be anywhere near the 'low bid' in an openly competitive environment– in both good and challenging times. He explained how a simple maintenance/service follow-up inspection and repair offer brings in huge referral and repeat business volumes (these observations are validated by other contractors).

I connected Sonny's ideas with my own experiences, where, with revitalized branding, in two years I turned a failing business into a publishing success story. Even though many competing print media publishers are laying off employees, pressed by the combination of Internet competition and the biting winds of economic recession, we are we are growing, adding new cities, markets and services each year.

Advertising is a small part of the branding (and construction marketing) picture

Our business earns 99 per cent of its revenue by selling advertising to architectural, engineering and construction businesses but most contractors waste their advertising dollars. I will advocate in the pages ahead that you should advertise carefully, and that in most situations – unless your business is larger and you can truly afford to be patient before you expect results — conventional paid advertising should be a small part of your marketing budget. You can advertise effectively and profitably, but you will only want to do it to support other, less expensive and more immediately effective marketing methodologies.

One reason most people get advertising wrong is that they advertise in the wrong places, at the wrong times and in the wrong volume. Never purchase advertising in a newspaper or on a radio station mainly because you like the publication's content or station's music or because the sales representative has an engaging personality. Make your choice because your advertising medium reflects and reaches the market you are seeking to serve. To succeed at advertising you will need the financial resources to absorb your mistakes, and patience to wait long enough to measure the the results. So use (paid) advertising sparingly if your marketing budget is small. When you grow you will find advertising is highly effective and can differentiate your business. But you need to be cautious and patient before investing the serious money effective conventional advertising requires.

Define your construction marketing strategies by your passions

Do you enjoy sports? Football, hockey, soccer? If you started your own business, your trade or profession may be your passion. Maybe you like the outdoors: Hunting, fishing, connecting with wildlife. Perhaps you enjoy social activities, lots of friends, and good parties. Or you are like me, who prefers quiet time, alone, with a good book or time with my family. Maybe you enjoy travel, or perhaps you enjoy 'cocooning.' I will advocate in the pages ahead that you can, and should, relate your marketing with your potential clients by doing more of what you enjoy doing and doing it well. In other words, your marketing should be fun.

Of course, in doing what you love, you should always respect your current, previous and potential clients' real interests. If you enjoy opera and your potential clients enjoy baseball, you won't get far by forcing your interest in opera on them. However, most of the time, you will find your interests at least in some key ways relate to the people you wish to serve. If they don't, you might be in the wrong business. Alternatively, you might simply need to find people around you who can do the connecting more effectively, while you do what you enjoy.

Of course, you should be wary when salespeople play to your interests. They are practising what we preach here, but your objective is to achieve marketing success for your own business – not fulfilling the marketing objective of the vendors selling you their services.

After you finish reading this first section, you'll see how by relating your passions with your clients' interests, you will achieve 75 to 80 per cent of what you need to be truly successful at construction industry marketing. Then apply the concepts in Part II to complete the picture. You will learn the importance of association membership, how to prepare and win bids, which bids to avoid, how to put the Internet to work for you, and when and if advertising, canvassing, and leads services can help your business.

Employee or owner: Two perspectives

This book is written primarily from the perspective of the business owner hoping to create a thriving business, or, in the recession, to ensure its survival. However, if you are an employee, you will also receive valuable insights from these pages. Your challenge will be to show your boss how the relationships between you and other employees, clients, and the your company's management are key elements in successful marketing.

If you apply the principles in this book, you will find your work is increasingly satisfying, and your employer will value your contributions even more. Your boss will also like the fact that most of the suggestions here do not require additional budget resources and, in fact, may save money on your day-to-day operations.

Subcontractor, supplier, architect, engineer, contractor – an interdisciplinary perspective

This book is designed to serve all of the disciplines and professions within the construction industry. Of course, your world view and specific marketing methods will vary depending on whether your business is taping drywall for homeowners or designing multi-million dollar convention centres. Nevertheless, if your business is small, most principles of effective marketing still apply. If you are employed in the marketing department at a large architectural or contracting business, I hope you will appreciate when you finish this book that "brand consistency" is a whole lot more than getting your logo dimensions correct.

How construction marketing can be simple and fun

As you read these pages, you will notice that I am advocating a different approach to construction industry marketing than you will find in many textbooks. You will discover ideas that are straightforward and easy to implement. You will have fun, even as you enhance your business profitability.

Chapter 2

Your brand: Why it is so important

You need to look hard on the map to find Courtland, Ontario, the home of Reid and Deleye, a mid-sized general contractor serving communities within a 50-mile radius of its offices near London, in southwestern Ontario. Reid and Deleye doesn't have a fancy website, great brochures, or a modern logo, but after a few hours working with company vice-president Greg Eyre and his staff, you know they've achieved branding – and marketing — success.

We were profiling Reid and Deleye in a special feature article in *Ontario Construction Report*. A good sign that this company's brand is excellent is that dozens of suppliers, without questioning the value of their marketing investment, quickly agreed to support the feature with their own advertising contributions.

We publish dozens of these features each year, but Reid and Deleye stood out from the crowd. I immediately noticed some important positive distinctions about this business. For example, I noticed how Greg Eyre, in working with me on the feature article, covered the essential ground quickly and efficiently and reviewed changes and proofs at a speed that I've rarely seen. His staff were equally quick in responding to our requests to facilitate the feature. (I believe if you were a client or sub trade working with Reid and Deleye, you would receive exactly the same attention and responsiveness.)

Later, suppliers and other contractors agreed with this perception: Hundreds of people voted in favor of Reid and Deleye as the *Ontario Construction Report's* 2008-2009 Readers Choice Award Gold winner.

Your great brand – it is all about trust

Reid and Deleye, in fact, has achieved true branding success. They have developed the speedy and relationship-focused responsiveness that allows clients, employees and suppliers to conduct business effectively and rapidly. Most importantly, through their actions, they have earned trust — the cornerstone of truly great brands.

Branding is the perception, backed by real experiences of current and previous clients, that you will deliver genuine value and satisfaction. With brand trust, you can command higher prices and earn a reasonable profit for your work.

Knowing your brand

You may already have a great brand but not be conscious of your success. For example, your clients know you deliver your services with the highest integrity and quality. They bring repeat business, and refer their friends. However, if you are like many contractors and professionals, you may price your services like a commodity. You think that the "lowest price wins the job" and you must be competitive. In other words, you under-value (and often under-price) your services.

Your goal in marketing your construction business is to understand and elevate your brand's value. As its value increases you will capture even higher prices and margins. When your brand is well above average, you will command a significant premium over price-focused competition. Clearly, if you can charge more for your services than the competition, your profits will be higher. (And if you have a great brand, but only now are realizing this fact, you will see your margins skyrocket when you learn how to price your services at their true value.)

Client trust that is truly earned and reflected in your business brand is worth thousands or even millions of dollars.

Branding and the real world

Of course, market conditions change. In slow economies, desperate people, even contractors with good brands, bid low to survive. This is usually a mistake. Equally, some people think that it makes sense to chase public bidding opportunities that are supposedly assessed objectively. You may think that if you put in the best bid, you will win.

However, the real world is much different. For example, I recall speaking with a midwestern contractor who consistently submitted low bids for a local hospital and always won. The contractor and the hospital staff had a mutual understanding that their scope-of-work definitions would allow for profitable change orders. So the contractor always bid low on the public tenders, and the hospital managers approved the pre-arranged change orders, and thus the contractor's profits.

Some might think this practice unethical. However, the legitimate basis for these unofficial understandings is that the contractor's brand is strong enough. Having worked together on many projects, the hospital and contractor's staff trust, respect and relate well to each other, and know the projects will not only succeed, but also fall within the true budget objectives.

Your marketing goal should be to achieve similar branding success, not just with one client but with many. Then your business will thrive in good and bad economies.

Earning the brand trust

To achieve branding success, you must earn this higher level of trust. With trust comes clients' confidence in you. They won't worry about your price because they know they will be treated fairly and receive real value.

Note that successful branding is not primarily about advertising, logo design, and marketing materials. The most important elements in your business are your client relationships and their experiences with your employees.

If you have enjoyed lasting success in business, your brand is undoubtedly good. For example, if you are like the majority of contractors and architects who earn most of their business through repeat and referral enquiries, you have reached the point where your current and previous clients trust you enough both to return for more and to recommend friends and colleagues. That's the sign of a healthy brand. So your challenge is to improve on a good thing. In later chapters, I'll show you how and why.

If, on the other hand, you don't have repeat and referral business, and you are always chasing jobs with the lowest bid price, you may have underlying business problems. You will need to attend to them before you start advertising, promoting and marketing your company.

Branding: Passion and leadership

You'll find that your achievement of a more successful brand relates closely to your personality and passions – and those of your employees in their interactions with each other and your clients. Outstanding business success usually starts with the excitement, talent and passion of the founder and then radiates through the company's employees.

Great branding is the sum of all the experiences your clients have with your business – from the receptionist's greeting to the way your staff handle final inspection and clean-up.

Brand Harmony and your business culture

Steve Yastrow's book, *Brand Harmony*, provides some essential insights into effective branding. At first glance, this book is far removed from the construction industry. Yastrow's examples relate more to the consumer and hospitality industries.

Taking an example from Yastrov, let's say you arrive at a hotel expecting to have a comfortable room, a restful evening, and then perhaps a great day with your family or some solid business meetings. Instead, you encounter long line ups at check-in, less-than-enthusiastic clerks, and your room isn't quite as it appears in the brochures or the hotel's website. Perhaps you will tolerate the place. Maybe there isn't another convenient hotel at the price range nearby. You might stay at that hotel again, but you won't rave about it and you won't feel any satisfaction. You may well say the place is terrible. You may even share the bad news with friends, family and business colleagues.

Although the details may differ, the same issues apply to architectural, engineering and construction companies. Perhaps the two biggest complaints — and the easiest to fix – are complaints about unreturned phone calls and messy job sites.

Of course, there are other aspects of your company that may affect well or poorly on your clients or suppliers. Are your employees cheerful, respectful, responsive, and do they genuinely enjoy their work?

Do clients have the impression that you grudgingly do the bare minimum to "get by" or do they sense you are truly interested in their project? The interactions you and your colleagues have with your clients reflect your overall attitudes to everyone around you, including your suppliers and subcontractors.

Branding is individual and client-centric

Branding is an individual, client-centric thing – it is not some "marketing department" stuff. It is the sum total of interactions between your business and its clients.

(*Construction Marketing Ideas* blog entry, 2007)

In an email to me, Sonny Lykos wanted to get the marketing and branding message to contractors who struggled to get by, earning little money for much work. He observed:

"(Branding is) what I call the strongest foundation in the world – what an inverted pyramid rests upon. For these highly successful companies, it's the founder of the business, or rather his character, personality and the culture he creates around him, like an aura.

"That aura is the foundation from which the company grows and spreads during its growth. And that aura is infectious only to others with the same philosophy. And then they, in turn, also attract other like-minded people as the company grows.

"It is the perfect example, and defines the term, 'brand harmony.' Hard to create such a business. Harder yet to maintain the reasons for its success. For these companies' employees, (brand harmony) does, as you surmised, 'come naturally.'"

Discovering your brand

To achieve construction marketing success, you have to discover and develop your brand. I advocate achieving branding success by capturing your own passions and strengths, sharing these with your employees and clients and encouraging the same level of work satisfaction and accomplishment among the people who work with you every day.

Once you appreciate the good brand you already have, or learn how to develop it, you'll be ready for more advanced marketing strategies. However, you must ensure your brand is healthy first.

How do you clients see you?

The late Sonny Lykos, who advocated building your brand by looking closely at all your client interactions and making sure you always leave a positive impression, made these observations in a comment to the Construction Marketing Ideas *blog in December, 2007. His original remarks are edited for syntax and grammar, but his core message is timeless and relevant. Do you see your own business practices here?*

What is the standard by which contractors, both general and speciality, operate? Let me list just a few examples of standard operating procedures.

1. Phone calls are not returned promptly. How could they be when you're so busy doing other things. Hey, you run a business, right?
2. Cleanliness is not important. It's the "workmanship," not the residual debris that's important, right? Especially for plumbers and electricians.
3. So what if you show up a couple of hours (or days) later than the arranged time and day. You have problems like everyone else, right?
4. I know you look like you just changed your water pump, but hey! you've been working. And what does a haircut have to do with your work?
5. Never, ever, do anything for free. Even if it's good for marketing or PR, never forget you are in business to make money, not give it away.
6. Help other people if needed? Are you nuts! No one ever helped me with anything.

People who you've contracted with were late, slobs, didn't return your calls, looked like they just crawled out from under a rock, nickel and dimed you for everything, and never once offered to give you a hand when it was needed. So how did you like being treated not as a customer, but as a third-rate person?

It's funny when one expects others to apply the Golden Rule to them, but don't think of applying it by to their own customers as part of their company culture. After all, they're too busy running a business. And it's as simple as that - the Golden Rule. Take care of your customers, and their staff, as you would like to be WOW'd by those with whom you sign contracts.

Go ahead. Be an anomaly. I dare you! . . .

Successful people form the habit of doing the things failures don't like to do.

Lykos followed up with a second comment:

As I've stated before, most contractors, including speciality contractors, think with a tradesman mentality instead of a businessmen's mentality. And all too often, even those who think as a business person have the impression that "branding" is like advertising. Not so. Advertising and marketing only get the customer interested in the company. They are therefore, tempted to try their product, or in our case, service.

Branding is simply what the customer thinks of you. It's that simple. It's not a logo. It's not a discount. It's not "only" the calibre of your work. Their perception is based upon a compilation of every single contact anyone from your company has had with them, and believe it or not, that includes how those in the company answer the phone, what they say, and their manner.

Treat them in a manner that is the opposite of what they expect, and the opposite of what they expect because what they expect is the public's knowledge of the lousy reputation of our industry.

The key is to not just "satisfy" a customer. Many business do that, merely satisfy them. The key is to WOW each customer.

How do you attract most of your business?

In the past two years, hundreds of readers have responded to an ongoing poll in my *Construction Marketing Ideas* blog that asks the following question: How do you attract most of your new business?

Look at the results in order of significance:

Word of Mouth / Recommendations	38 per cent
Existing Clients	36 per cent
Leads services / RFPs / Public Tenders	11 per cent
Advertising	10 per cent
Canvassing / Telemarketing	5 per cent

Note the most important measure here: 74 per cent of work for most architectural, engineering and construction firms arises from word-of-mouth and repeat business. Clearly, any marketing initiative that stimulates more business in these two important categories will yield more and greater results than other marketing methods.

Your first marketing priorities

This doesn't mean the other resources should be ignored. In fact, they are essential for your company's growth. Nevertheless, you must carefully consider the cost and return on investment and time. Unless your business is truly exceptional, with a well-designed and effective advertising and marketing strategy, you should be cautious about using alternative marketing methods until you can get your repeat/referral business to the 74 per cent norms.

(If you are a start-up, or your referral and repeat business has dried up because of the economy, you need to be prudent about spending money on other forms of marketing which you haven't tested carefully. First look carefully at your previous and current client base for ways to tap potential referrals and repeat clients.)

Small improvements: Big results

Say, for example, you focus your marketing to improve your repeat business by 10 per cent. If your business is typical, the result would be a gain of 3.6 per cent (10 per cent of 36 per cent) in overall business volume. Since you probably can achieve this incremental gain without significant cash spending, you will find the results contribute immediately to your bottom line. In fact, just a 10 per cent improvement in the combination of repeat and referral business would result in a net gain of 7.4 per cent in overall revenue, enough in many cases to make the difference between profit and loss.

Clearly then, your marketing priorities should start with an understanding of what it takes to ensure your clients are truly happy – even exuberant – with your service. You then need to tap into this enthusiasm to encourage repeat and referral orders. In the long term, nothing you do will pay off as effectively.

See Section II for more insights into how to enhance repeat and referral business and apply these tips before implementing any other marketing strategies.

Chapter 3

Your strengths, passions, and enjoyment are keys to your marketing success

Imagine, for a moment, the perfect world where you and all of your employees truly enjoy your work. Everyone starts the day with enthusiasm; you are not thinking of the time clock, or bi-weekly bank deposit; you are simply, totally and passionately immersed in your work.

The perfect world – following your strengths

In this world, your clients would be amazed by the skills of your staff, work quality, and capacity. They will want to give you plenty of additional work, or perhaps even join your organization as joint venture partners or employees. You've achieved marketing and business perfection.

This dream-come-true situation occurs more often than you might expect. You may have experienced a similar high in the early stages of your organization, or when you were working on the dream project. It's often apparent in successful, fast-growing businesses like Google, or among teams of craftspeople, who each day celebrate life with their passion and love of their work.

An architectural success story

To illustrate, Diane Valenti, director of marketing and business development at JMWA Architects in Boca Raton, Florida, tells her firm's story. Interviewed for an article in the *SMPS Marketer* about Public-Private Partnerships (P3), Valenti explained that it wasn't so much her marketing work but her practice's successful business relationships, that led to JMWA's major undertaking — designing five U.S. Citizenship and Immigration Services (CIS) building projects in South Florida under Federal P3 guidelines.

James Williams, JMWA principal and project architect, explained that the U.S. General Services Administration (GSA) posted a Solicitation for Offers for the new buildings, with points awarded for price, location of the site, quality of working relationships among the project proponents, and of course the actual building design. He said one of his clients, a local developer, had an unused site in the declining Florida real estate market. A Washington, D.C.-based developer, who knew about the GSA proposal, saw the site and encouraged JMWA's client to submit a proposal.

"We had just two weeks to meet the deadline," he said. "The developer asked if we would prepare our design proposal at cost, which was reasonable to us...we aren't interested in working with people who expect us to do the design work for free in hopes of winning the job but accepted that we wouldn't make a profit on the initial design if it failed to go further."

When CIS officials saw the design, "they loved it" so much that they encouraged the developer to scout out the other sites in South Florida to build similar buildings. As a result, JMWA designed five LEED Silver-certified buildings in less than two years.

In this case, as in most marketing success stories, JMWA won the initial opportunity because the clients trusted the practice. They knew JMWA had delivered in the past, so they were willing to pay a fee even if the project didn't get off the ground.

Passion, teamwork, and meeting the deadline

Imagine the mood in JMWA's offices as designers and support staff worked as a team to meet that very tight project deadline. They knew they would not be able to bill for overtime or extras, but nevertheless gave it their all because there was no doubt in their mind that they could succeed.

When you win the work as they did, you'll have reached that state of business near-perfection: Lots of profitable work, even in a challenging economy, with your success validated by your clients who engage your services again and again.

The other side of the coin

In contrast to the JMWA success story, consider this: You visit a supplier's workplace and experience a very different situation. Discontented people behind the counter barely grant you a smile; they are there because they have to be there. They do their job and get out. Employees are exhorted to try harder, to work more, and to solve the company's problems or they will lose their jobs. Everyone is tense, or lazy, distracted or angry.

Most of us have seen this type of workplace. If we decide to do business with this sort of company, it's because they have a monopoly (or have totally traded off any level of service for extremely low prices), or because our boss insists we work with them. Perhaps we are working with them through habit or because they do business with our own company and we feel obligated to support our clients.

Changing the story

The question is: Can you build passionate joy into your work, and that of your employees? And if you are an employee, can you change your own attitude and help to improve the working environment at your organization?

Yes, absolutely. Marcus Buckingham has written extensively about how to achieve these results. You can find more information at his website, TMBC (www.tmbc.com).

The idea of respecting your strengths provides some important insights into building your marketing success from within yourself and your organization, and is a core concept of this book. Your "strengths" are the combination of natural talent and passion or interest that propel you to work with intensity and improve consistently so you are a leader in your field.

Everyone has strengths: Can you discover them?

Buckingham advises both employees and managers to structure their jobs and their career paths around their strengths. He also encourages business owners or managers to rethink conventional job descriptions so that everyone in the organization can excel in their particular role in line with the business objectives.

Strengths: Consistency and energy

Buckingham writes that many companies rely on this motto: "Our company's greatest asset is our people!"

It's a nice motto, but it's meaningless without introspection and application. And the truth is, people aren't your greatest asset, unless they're in position to leverage their greatest strengths - those things they do well consistently and energetically.

Years of research prove that individuals and teams playing to their strengths significantly outperform those who don't in almost every business metric. In fact, the single best predictor of a consistently high-performing team is the answer to this question: "At work, do you have the opportunity to do what you do best everyday?" Teams with individuals who do massively outperform teams with people who don't. They're more profitable, more productive, less likely to quit, less likely to have accidents on the job...the list goes on.

That's compelling, but this is confounding: Our research reveals that only 12 per cent of people in the workplace play to their strengths "most of the time." In general, society is fascinated by weaknesses (most employee reviews bear this out), and we take strengths for granted.

At a time when organizations are trying to do more with fewer people, it's critical to engage each person's strengths, and do it at scale across the organization. The strengths movement isn't about making people happier; it's about making organizations more productive. It's about yield. The best companies are made up of great teams. And those teams have individuals who know their strengths, take them seriously and offer them up to the organization.

From **Why Strengths** *at* http://www.marcusbuckingham.com

There is much value in Buckingham's books, including his classic: *The One Thing You Need to Know* (Simon & Schuster, 2005). In it, he offers a road-map for setting your own career on track, and if you are an entrepreneur or business manager, a set of tools to help you reshape the culture and practices of your organization.

Your strengths allow you to overcome your weaknesses, without fighting them

My greatest strengths success story is intensely personal. Through my entire life, from childhood onwards, I have not been gifted with great social or interpersonal relationship skills. Bullies picked on me in grade school, and in high school I belonged to the "out group." How would I ever find my way to live a healthy, balanced life?

I did have a talent for writing and had a fascination with journalism. At university, I joined the student newspaper and began to learn the craft. With limited social skills, I had an uphill battle, but I loved my work, learned how to interview people, and how to compose stories quickly and well. Nevertheless, I still couldn't function effectively in most social environments.

Seeing the world: Seeing myself

One of my strengths and passions has been understanding the confluence of geography and history. After graduating from university, I set out for Africa and eventually, became a sub-editor on a newspaper in Bulawayo, in the year that Rhodesia won its independence and became Zimbabwe, ending a 10-year civil war.

Thus, I had achieved my dream. I had become a foreign correspondent and made journalism my career.

Returning to reality

When I came back to Canada in 1980, I returned to a recession. Several Canadian newspapers had closed and hundreds of experienced journalists lost their jobs. So I supported myself by cleaning the garbage and trays at McDonalds, meanwhile looking for something a little better. At a government employment office, the counsellor wasted no time offering me a job with his own department. Within months, the department transferred me to Ottawa to a then high-paying job as a civil servant, writing news releases and brochures.

While this job paid well and I could do it competently, it certainly didn't relate at all to my strengths, my passions and my true interests.

Connecting the dots: Discovering your real strengths

Eventually, I summoned the courage to quit my well-paid government job and I set out to sell real estate. Friends and family thought I was nuts. Why go from a secure job to a field that seemed totally unsuited for me? But I had a gut feeling that the choice would take me where I needed to go. Within two years I was ready and had enough raw-guts sales experience to go into business for myself.

First, I started a publication for real estate agents, and then, a couple of years later, established a newspaper for local construction contractors. This became the foundation of my publishing business. My company now operates in several cities in both Canada and the U.S., reflecting my life-long interest in diversity and international travel.

Our strengths are not the same

We all are different – the key to great business (and marketing) success is to respect, recognize, and then capture your own strengths and those of your employees. You may be a much better golfer or hockey player than writer; you may have highly developed social skills and enjoy being with friends. You may be a great cook, or yachter, or engineer. We are all different. Your challenge is to capture your strengths and use these as your driving force in business development and marketing, You will then be able to work around your weaknesses where they might otherwise limit your opportunity for success.

Building on strengths is much better than solving weaknesses

Stories of how heroes overcome weaknesses and achieve success despite the odds make great film or television dramas, but they rarely represent the best way to do things. You might want to be a pro-basketball player, but unless you are tall and have natural athletic ability, you will likely be disappointed. However, if you are a pro-level player, you may need to build your team-support skills to achieve your true talent and potential.

Conversely, you might be really good at doing some things that you hate. Do you really enjoy your current career? Alternatively, you might enjoy a sport or hobby in which you can never expect to be the greatest talent. Certainly you can and should play in house league games for your own enjoyment. You would not want your business and marketing to be focused in either of these directions, however. Instead, in your business and career, you want to capture the right mix of enjoyment and passion. If you aren't good at something, don't enjoy it or lack talent, you will be wise to stop and assess the situation. Determine if you really need to do the things you dislike or if you can find someone with the strengths to take them over.

Your employees' strengths are vital for your marketing success

Once you have ensured you are using your own strengths and passions to succeed, you need to tackle the more difficult challenge of ensuring your entire organization has the same spirit. This of course is not an easy or simple change to make, even if you are the owner and primary decision-maker, and may prove to be an uphill battle if you are a middle-manager or technical or marketing employee.

In truly successful businesses, most employees enjoy their work and are well-placed to communicate their passion and career satisfaction to colleagues and current and potential clients.

However, you cannot force other people to change. Long established traditions and relationships and employees who don't want to change may permeate your organization and make quick improvements virtually impossible.

The recession solution

You probably don't want to have to implement the solution that I discovered. In the middle part of the decade, most of our business's employees were disgruntled, disappointed and didn't really want to work at their jobs. Our sales and business declined precipitously to the point that, to survive, I needed to dismiss virtually everyone. This bad news fortunately gave me the opportunity to get back to my writing and journalism passions and much closer to our clients, and allowed the business to recover. Now, new employees only join our company after a thorough and careful selection process which we work hard to ensure they are truly right for their careers.

In a recession, you may have the perfect opportunity for some house cleaning. You will probably be wise to dismiss employees who are hanging on for the money, rather than their passion and skill. As your organization shrinks, it will also become stronger with people who truly enjoy and care about their work. No one likes throwing employees out of their jobs especially in hard times, but you can create a much healthier business if you streamline your operations for your best and most passionate colleagues.

Leading by example

The other, slower, approach to building a healthy organization is to lead by example. Follow your own strengths and passions and build opportunities wherever you can. As things progress, you may find your colleagues and managers see what is happening, and you can get them to buy into the program. You may also discover it is time to set out on your own or to join another organization more closely aligned to your own values.

You may of course not be able to change everything instantly. You can control some aspects of your working environment. Taking some small steps to reduce irritants and to increase work satisfaction will make time at work much more enjoyable and effective. Your clients will see the change, too.

When you and your employees wake up each morning in a state of mental bliss where you look forward with anticipation to your work, to stretching your abilities, and reaching the highest levels possible of accomplishment in your endeavours, you'll reach the magical point which virtually assures business and marketing success. Your current clients will want to do more business with you and you'll attract the new clients you are seeking.

Resources for determining your strengths

Tom Rath's *StrengthsFinder 2.0* (Gallup Press 2007) includes an online test to help you to discover your strengths. Marcus Buckingham has also published several books on this topic. These resources are helpful, but you may already know where your natural strengths lie.

Your childhood interests

Think back to your middle childhood and your memories of what you really enjoyed doing, and did well. Perhaps you enjoyed sports, hanging out with friends, or reading. (I started a neighbourhood newspaper, an early sign that journalism could be my ideal career.)

Blissful moments

Most of us can recall being so absorbed in our work that we don't think of time. We are on a natural high. This is common among tradespeople and professionals who really enjoy their work, people who choose their careers from love rather than money. As a writer, I find I thrive at 5 a.m. at the computer keyboard with a cup of coffee and silence around me. Without much effort, words form into sentences, sentences into paragraphs, and articles turn into the book you are reading now. Capture your bliss and you have likely found your strengths.

Validation from others

When I told my family that I wanted to start a publishing business, I recall my mother saying, without hesitation: "I'll give you some money to get started." You've captured your strengths when you not only enjoy your work, but the people around you also acknowledge that you have found your natural talent and wish to help you along.

Respecting employees' strengths

Many business people spend a great deal of time helping weaker employees overcome their problems, rather than supporting stronger employees to achieve their fullest potential. However, your business will be much healthier if you focus on your stronger employees and help them develop their abilities, rather than worrying about the weaker ones by trying to train them to fit in.

You may find that weaker employees are doing work unsuited to their natural ability and not fully developing their strengths. By encouraging them to redefine their work so that they tap into their natural abilities and passions, they will regain enthusiasm and enjoyment in the tasks at hand. Both your clients and your company's bottom line will benefit.

The same remedy applies to high performing employees who may be doing their job well, but don't really enjoy their work. If you can redeploy them so that they are enthusiastic and happy about their work, your business will have much more productivity and energy. You will soon find your marketing is much more successful, as well because current and potential clients will find your employee enthusiasm and positive spirit infectious and appealing.

Construction Marketing Ideas *blog, Wednesday, June 11, 2008*

Hard work or working hard?

Today, after an intense day in Toronto and Welland, I mused on one of the biggest paradoxes of work. If you try too hard, you will fail. If you don't work hard enough, you will fail, too. You need to work hard, but for it not to be work — in other words, you need to enjoy what you do so much that you can put your energy, time, heart and resourcefulness to the task(s) at hand.

If you are fortunate enough to be in these circumstances, you also know how your work/vocation correlates and complements your overall life. Happy at work, you are often happier at home. And if you are not happy at home, you may well not be happy at work — and that can set off a downward spiral.

Your passions count

How does this impact your approach to business, and marketing? First, if you are doing this work because it is a "job" and not really your passion, you may wish to move on. Indeed a lot of people employed in the marketing departments at AEC firms "move on" within a couple of years. This is borne out by the turnover in membership at the Society for Marketing Professional Services. (And it isn't too surprising, in that few young people grow up with dreams of being a proposal writer, business development officer, or "rainmaker.")

Moving on, by the way, doesn't necessarily mean going to your boss and saying "Take this job and shove it. I quit." Much more simply, it could be just reviewing the parts of the work you enjoy/like doing the most, and the parts you like the least, and with your organization's support, finding a way to spend more time on what you enjoy and less on what you distaste.

Are you there just for the money?

If you are the boss or supervisor, your perspective should parallel this approach — if your employees are just there for the money and really hate their work, your brand is sure to suffer. Surely, discontented employees will radiate their lack of enthusiasm to the clients, and we know that current clients provide most of your future business, either through repeat business or referrals.

This thinking can operate on another level, as well. I find I achieve the most selling success when I seemingly don't really try to sell. In my case, the sales often result when I practice my journalistic passion. So I go out and talk to people, and interview them, and attend events, and write stories, and amazingly, it seems, business almost drops into my lap as if by accident. Of course it isn't totally accidental — at just the right moment, in these circumstances, I know to ask for the order and usually get it.

Meeting the real quota

But I would be really depressed if I needed to wake up each morning and "make calls" and "meet the quota." I might be able to sell, quite effectively at times, but I don't want to be a salesperson.

Now some people indeed are suited for "sales careers" and they find it natural to work with the discipline and structure — and single minded focus — to bring in the orders, all the time. There are other salespeople who seem to achieve their results almost effortlessly, perhaps because they focus on the relationship process (even better than I do), and, like me, know when it is right to ask for the business.

My advice to you (with thanks to the work of Marcus Buckingham) is to encourage you to take stock of your own passions, energy, and those of your peers, and employees. Find your own spark, respect that of the people around you, and you'll likely succeed, regardless of the external environment.

Chapter 4

The 76/24 rule for AEC marketing: Systems for repeat and referral business development

You may be aware of the Pareto principle, which says that 80 per cent of the results in most endeavours comes from 20 per cent of the causes. Business management thinker Joseph M. Juran suggested the principle and named it after Italian economist Vilfredo Pareto, who observed that 80 per cent of income in Italy went to 20 per cent of the population. It is a common rule-of-thumb in business; e.g., "80 per cent of your sales comes from 20 per cent of your clients."

Our own research shows similar results when assessing the biggest sources of new business from architectural, engineering and construction (AEC) services.

In chapter 2, I reported on these results from my *Construction Marketing Ideas* blog poll, but I am repeating them here because of their importance.

How do you attract new business?

Word-of-mouth or referrals	38%
From existing clients	36%
Leads services/RFP/Public Tenders	11%
Advertising	10%
Canvassing/Telemarketing	5%

Combined, word-of-mouth (referrals) and existing clients generate 74 per cent of business for the hundreds of people who have participated in the blog's online poll with 24 per cent from other sources (the 76/24 rule.) This tells us a couple of important things:

1. Anything you do to improve referral and repeat business quality and volume will have disproportionate value in improving your business results; and
2. Any failure in retaining clients or engagement in business practices that cause negative word-of-mouth should be regarded as a red-flag crisis.

The exception proves the rule

Paradoxically, the Pareto principle also suggests that if you are one of the 26 per cent of construction businesses who attract most of their clients through methods other than word-of-mouth and repeat business, you may have a distinct competitive – and marketing – advantage. Why? Because you have broken away from the pack and you own a space in the marketing area others find difficult to enter. For example, Mike Feazel, President of Feazel Roofing in Columbus, Ohio, says his company spends upwards of $200,000 a year on radio advertising, and finds at least a third of its business that way. A second third is from repeat/referrals, and the remaining third is from everything else, he says.

"We can't get to this stage of being the largest roofing contractor in Ohio without going beyond word-of-mouth and referral marketing," he says.

He also points out that it takes money and time to make the radio advertising work. It requires several months of concentrated, repeat advertising for it to pay off. However, you are unlikely to want to risk your resources learning how to advertise this way, especially if your cash is tight. Few competitors would dare try to emulate Feazel's example, and it is this barrier to competitive response that gives him a different kind of 80/20 advantage.

The 76/24 solution for the majority

If you are like most architectural, engineering and construction companies, you will only break away from the 74/26 rule with great caution, because rashly going outside the primary source of repeat/referral business could dig you into a deep hole, very quickly. Too many contractors rush to advertise in a business downturn, but they may not have the experience to determine which forms of advertising will work the best, nor do they have the patience and resources for trial-and-error solutions.

So, although successful contractors like Mike Feazel and consultants such as Michael Stone advocate relying less on repeat/referral business and more on alternative approaches to business development that are outside your comfort zone, you need to think about these measures carefully and thoughtfully. If you are just starting a formal marketing program, I believe your first, and most important, strategy is to systematize your repeat and referral marketing communications and practices to increase your yield from them.

Beware of relying on, rather than managing your repeat/referral business

Most business people who say they rely on repeat business and word-of-mouth referrals simply think the good times can continue forever. However, when conditions change, companies without systems and processes to generate repeat and referral business can find things dry up. Worse, you may find you have two or three clients generating most of your business (the 76/24 rule again), and when one or more of them fails or leaves for greener pastures, you are in big trouble.

You need a different approach here, a systematic, planned, thought-though and tested series of steps, actions and procedures to encourage, entice, attract and build on the repeat/referral business volume. These measures don't need to be obtrusive or "in your face," but they should be incorporated into everything you do.

Maintaining contact with current and previous clients

A key strategy to enhance your repeat and referral business is to maintain regular contact with both current and previous clients. You need unobtrusive yet consistent strategies here, Nevertheless, you'll find keeping in touch is probably your most effective marketing strategy.

Some ways to maintain regular contact with your current and previous clients are:

- **Electronic newsletters:** Surprisingly inexpensive, and with new technologies, easy to maintain and update.
- **Your blog:** With a blog you build credibility and a fan base; and (for new client development) your search engine ranking really rises.
- **Association involvement where your clients are located:** My favourite, because you gain credibility and build on existing relationships and referrals in a face-to-face environment.
- **Christmas cards and other seasonal greetings:** The hand-written note really helps; rather than mass card mailings, use the personal touch.
- **Friendly follow-up phone conversations and visits:** Especially useful if you have something of value to provide your client. Don't worry about the sale, this is about keeping in touch.
- **Community and charitable events and activities:** These give you the opportunity to invite the participation of your current or former clients without a direct, in-your-face, sales pitch.

- **Business lunches or breakfasts**
- **Complementary tickets to cultural or sporting events**

Some third-party vendors and internet services offer "follow-up services" which will systematize and report on e-letters and mailings; these can be valuable, but should not be a substitute for your own direct connection and interaction with previous clients.

Combining staff and client interests and passions

I believe you achieve the most effective marketing results when your employees connect their own interests with their clients. You can formalize some rules such as requiring every representative to send a personal thank-you card to each new client or set up regular communication programs that systematize the follow-up process, perhaps using some simple third-party services to co-ordinate it. However, the best approach, I believe, is to give your employees room to be themselves. Allow them a modest budget and invite them to devise their own solutions.

Since most architectural, engineering and construction projects are intense, long-term initiatives, they offer wonderful opportunities for connecting with clients and receiving feedback while the projects are under way. Of course, out of these relationships, you can build an information bank for future projects, referrals, or opportunities to gain intelligence that may lead to new work.

More typically, however, when a project ends, you move on, and so do your clients. Unless you have an ongoing relationship and they have an ongoing need, you risk losing touch with them.

Structured follow-up service programs

In order to capitalize on already-established working relationships, you may want to build in some scheduled follow-up service and support beyond any contractual warranty provisions. Your incremental costs for building in service and maintenance calls is relatively small and will easily be paid back with positive brand recognition, client loyalty, and on-the-spot referrals. Imagine if you offer a warranty two or three times longer than industry standard on the condition you can complete follow-up inspections and remedy problems. You have created a built-in selling advantage up front AND solid relationships going forward.

If you don't currently have a follow-up system in place with extra service or warranty coverage, you may be losing your single most effective marketing resource available to your business.

Develop an inspection and maintenance service call system

Contractors report that follow-up inspection and maintenance calls can be very profitable. Here are the reasons:

1. **You gain an up-front selling advantage.** Guarantee your services beyond the norm and promise a follow-up call or maintenance visit before even starting the job; your clients have one less thing to worry about.
2. **When you carry out the maintenance inspection and service call, you are showing you deliver on your promises.** At the same time, you can reassure your clients that they are making the best of their purchase. At that point, some may elect to buy ongoing service contracts. Others may ask you to do additional work for them.
3. **This follow-up system makes it easier for you to measure your success.** You can audit your work quality and measure real client satisfaction without artificial or forced surveys.

Incentive programs for repeat and referral business

In addition to structured follow-up visits, consider the advantage of incentive programs for repeat and referral business. This can be as simple as a formal discount for "second visits," not unreasonable, since you don't have to pay the marketing costs. Alternatively, you can offer a small cash incentive for referrals.

Consider the approach used by Feazel Roofing in Columbus, Ohio. The company offers a $50 cash referral fee to the individual making the referral, and an additional $50 savings for the new client. Additionally, there is a profit-building enhancement: The referral form allows whoever makes the referral to sign over their $50 to the recipient, resulting in a $100 savings to the person actually using the coupon. Some friends or relatives are not going to want to seem so cheap as to claim the $50 in cash so they sign the form over, turning a hard cash cost into a soft $50 services discount. Of course, with these forms, Feazel Roofing can easily track and measure the volume of referral business the program generates.

Another note on the 74/26 rule: When to offload your problems

The corollary of using the 74/26 rule in your marketing is knowing when NOT to market. By eliminating the least profitable 26 per cent of your activities and clients, your business productivity and profit will skyrocket. For example, when you review your request for proposal (RFP) process, consider where you are having the lowest success/hit rate. You have two choices; you can decline to bid further projects in this sector, or rethink your process. In many cases, it is wisest simply to decline, and then devote your energies where you have better results.

The same applies for current clients. Some don't pay their bills, consume inordinate amounts of your management and team energy, and generate all-round bad karma. Drop them, or refer them to organizations where they may be served better.

Some brutal businesspeople also suggest getting rid of the bottom 20 per cent of your employees. Far more effective is creating a working environment where 80 per cent of your employees perform in the top 20 per cent of their field, reflecting their interests, passions and values. Then watch the remaining 20 per cent who simply don't fit find a way to leave sooner than later (and you won't need to pay hefty severance costs.)

Caution about your 24 per cent superstars

Equally risky is to focus your attention and respect on the top 20-24 per cent of your sales representatives. Over-relying on a few superstars can demoralize and demotivate the rest of your team, or, worse, push you into business practices which are against your best interests.

I learned the cost of this management flaw the hard way. At one time, our company's top salesperson could bring in an incredible amount of business, working just a few hours a week, and almost all on the phone without any direct client contact. She had truly efficient and powerful persuasive abilities.

Other salespeople gave up to her power. Even worse, clients and industry associations became alienated from the business because she turned every relationship into a money-finding activity. Her success proved costly to the business and its brand. It took years to overcome the resulting backlash.

As well, if you are really relying a few people out of many to generate 74 to 80 per cent of your business, what happens if they decide to leave? Your business will sink, and quickly.

Consider the balance:
Applying the 74/26 rule in practice

Clearly, the evidence shows that you should fully respect and manage the 74/26 rule and that you should give priority in your marketing to expanding your repeat and referral business. However, you also need to go beyond relying on these two important sources of business, especially if you wish to ensure viability of your business in hard times and grow when times are good.

If nothing else, you should devote at least 24 per cent of your business energy to building alternatives to your existing repeat and referral business. This will ensure you have the capacity to replenish the established clients who may leave for any reason. Note that when moving beyond the primary repeat/referral enhancement strategies in your marketing, your costs per lead and risk of failure will likely be much higher.

In other words, make systematic enhancement of your repeat and referral business your number one priority, but not your only one. You may need to pay for some expensive trial-and-error marketing while discovering methods beyond the obvious. In later chapters, I'll share some ideas that should help to reduce your risks.

Service follow-up – Some examples

Leonard Megliola, President of Bestline Plumbing in the Los Angeles area, challenges other contractors and sub trades to think differently about marketing; in the process, he has adapted and implemented some resourceful practices.

One of his methodologies, also recommended by the late Sonny Lykos, is the follow-up service/warranty inspection call. When his company completes a project, clients are advised that his staff will inspect their work a year after it is completed and make things right if they aren't up to standard.

His employees complete the inspections as promised, and obviously take responsibility to fix any deficiencies, but these visits have much more marketing power than meet the eye. Clients need additional things done; they also have friends and acquaintances who need plumbing services. Thus good-will created by the follow-up service just adds to this initiative's marketing value.

Megliola explained his system in the following Contractor Talk forum posting. (We've edited the actual posting for grammar and word-flow; Megliola acknowledges he is a plumber, not a writer.)

The way this campaign works is too simple. You send 100 letters to customers you did large jobs for. They could be room additions, foundation walls, copper pipes, furnaces, roofs, roof valleys, sewers, drain installations, electrical wiring, and so on.

Your letter tells your customer that you guaranteed your work, and you want to inspect it. If there is a problem, you will repair it for free.

People love this idea. We send out 100 letters and the phones start to ring the next day. Almost every customer we inspect needs something, and we are closing very large sales on 50 per cent of our inspections. This week, we sold three floor furnaces, some drain jobs, a copper re-pipe, and a huge clean-up job in an attic removing blown-in insulation that was contaminated with animal waste.

The first thing we do when arriving at the customer's home is to hand them some free pens and a few business cards. We carry a camera and take pictures of everything. If we find that nothing is wrong, we smile and thank the customer. When something is wrong, we do our best to repair it. This past Monday, we inspected six jobs in less than two hours. I prefer not to mention the amount of money sold from inspections, but it is more than most will believe . . . .

You should be willing to provide a complementary "check up service" as part of good customer relationships in order to build your business.

Client Relationship Management (CRM) Systems – Risks and Rewards

Can Client Relationship Management (CRM) software help you manage your client relationships, improve business efficiency, and enhance your marketing effectiveness? Yes, if you do it right, but far too few businesses succeed.

The reason is that the process of developing and maintaining the client database can turn into a bureaucratic nightmare, can result in "gaming" to ensure the results that your employees perceive you want, and can separate common-sense human relations and respect from your marketing priorities.

However, if you handle it correctly, solid CRM systems can improve your employee accountability, simplify your measurement of marketing initiatives, and enhance client service, especially if you track sensitive and useful touch-points and memories.

Rory Swan of Servicz Unlimited in Washington, D.C., for example observed in a Remodel Crazy posting:

"My software ranks the customer from the day the lead is first entered and changes, based on factors. We capture the types of projects that come our way. We also look at what jobs are more profitable than others.

"We use the data collection as a way to market to lost bids and follow up with potential clients.

"We enter the data in so that template letters can go out, that have enough customer info for them to seem personalized to that person, but not be difficult to produce."

Good CRM can tell you:
• What jobs are profitable;
• How customer found you;
• What marketing avenues are working and what is the cost of acquisition;
• Did a past client send you any referrals, what was the result of the referral;
• A data base for marketing and promotions.

"I keep a five year log (as) most homes here are sold and renovated every five years."

Swan also says his CRM records include a maintenance database to follow up on warranties and new sales opportunities.

Most contractors can cobble together a simple CRM system using their existing email and database software. Some companies provide turn-key systems and you can assess whether these will work for you; however of course be careful about locking into arrangements until you are satisfied they are right.

You can also consider inexpensive or free software on the Internet. George Zarogiannis of Ecopainting Inc. in Toronto recommends Zoho

CRM (available at www.zoho.com), for example. I've used this software to in manage the lead flow for inquiries from my *Construction Marketing Ideas* blog. Zoho CRM is free for three or fewer users, or you can obtain a slightly upgraded service for $12.00 per month per additional user. (That means, if you have four users, you would be able to use the upgraded system for $12.00 per month, without any contract requirements.) You should have some facility and comfort with computer databases and software to use this service.

Remember, of course, that CRM systems should not replace your personal connections and "touch" with your clients; CRM software is a tool, not a replacement, for great relationships and client service.

Chapter 5
Putting the pieces together with a business plan

Meetings and budgets

You've read about the importance of brand development, of encouraging your employees to excel at their strengths, and the vital importance of enhancing your business based on repeat and referral relationships, while strategically using the other marketing resources. Your challenge is to organize this process, without creating a bureaucracy. For this you will need a business plan and a systematic approach to communicating and connecting with your employees. Without it, you'll be travelling blind, even bouncing from one crisis to another. Even if your skills and talents bring an abundance of referral business, you won't have an effective way to deal with crises or surprises without a business plan. Without some process for management control and communication, your employees will head off in their own self-interested directions, without connecting their work to the overall business objectives.

The planning and meeting paradox

Most conventional business and marketing textbooks advocate that you develop and implement a business plan. For years, I balked at this, and now some scholars agree that the conventional approaches to business planning don't work especially well. The comprehensive written business plans produced by management consultants may look good on paper, but quickly gather dust.

On a separate level, but related to the business planning process, most larger businesses are overwhelmed by meetings. When we meet clients who work at some major corporations, they complain about the long, unnecessary, and excessive number of business meetings which drain energy, waste time, and achieve little in productive results.

For years, I refused to develop a formal business plan for my company, and when we had meetings, they were sporadic and for special purposes only.

Big mistake. This seat-of-the-pants approach created an environment where business development was defined by the strong-willed and selfish needs of individual employees. An example of the then-company culture was when I called a meeting to address some troubling business issues, and an out-of-town junior employee lobbied hard to attend, saying he had something useful to contribute. I allowed myself to be persuaded, and paid his travel costs. It turned out that his real reason for coming to town was to press the case for a salary increase for himself!

A different approach – All employees build the business plan

I am thankful to Bill Caswell of Caswell Corporate Coaching Company for teaching me the basics of how to structure the planning process.

The key to Caswell's business meeting and business planning methodology is a combination of structure, routine, and 100 per cent employee involvement. Employees share, review, and participate directly in the business plan development and in the setting of annual budgets. They all have the opportunity to participate, and everyone understands the resulting plan because they have helped to develop it. When things are falling off track, trouble-shooting or special planning meetings are easy to co-ordinate.

The "crisis" planning meeting

When my business experienced a survival crisis, Caswell asked me to convene an urgent planning meeting. We gathered in a chalet in West Quebec, about an hour's drive from our Ottawa home base. All employees were required to attend, at company expense. The session would last a full day; it could go overtime into the evening; and we would not wrap up until we solved the problems.

You could see the company's internal difficulties at the meeting; many of the staff (both employees and contractors) didn't want to be there; they didn't like each other or management. Additionally, they had to help me solve what seemed to be an insolvable challenge: Haemorrhaging business losses, defecting clients and hostility to our business from some major industry associations.

At the meeting, some of our newer employees, including a summer student, contributed some of the best ideas. These included a strategy to renew and build on sales of directory listings that successfully raised $20,000 in a few weeks, and is now part of our annual sales cycle. Other ideas were folded into a new business plan, and we pushed forward to survive.

Regular meetings – quick and routine

Caswell also helped us set up our regular meeting system. All of our employees and key contractors get together in the office and/or by teleconference once a week, for a meeting that cannot go longer than one hour. We are usually finished in 30 to 40 minutes. An agenda is prepared for each meeting, and meetings start and finish on time. Any employee can add or contribute to the agenda. At the beginning of each meeting, "action items" from previous meetings are reviewed and as the meeting progresses, new items are added to the list. Salary and individual performance issues are not discussed directly, but attendees gain clues about issues or problems that will be addressed one-on-one.

In addition to this general meeting, we have a weekly sales meeting, and to supplement the annual planning session, we have built in a mid-year-review, which again brings together all employees from wherever they may be.

The meeting turn-around process

In hindsight, the planning and meeting system saved our business, because it helped us to make tough and challenging decisions.

Other excellent elements about Caswell's planning process include simple systems that allow all of the company's key employees and contractors to participate in business planning development. Hence, they buy into the results. If they don't, then they usually choose to leave. Management doesn't spend endless hours arguing over fine points; employees don't have a top-heavy plan forced on them against their will.

With all expenses covered (including travel costs and per-diems or hourly pay for individuals who would suffer income loss otherwise by attending), the employees and contractors now look forward to the meetings.

Responding quickly to changes

The weekly meetings, meanwhile, allow us to adapt our plan to current circumstances. We can review progress of action items set at the major meetings and resolve current problems or concerns quickly and openly. I've also learned to detect warning signs that arise in the meetings. For instance, absence without a good reason is a major red flag; inconsistent behaviour or awkward communication is a yellow flag warning. In one case, I sensed something wrong and implemented protective measures. In fact, the employee had violated several company guidelines and had started to offend our clients. The individual left voluntarily within five days.

Rules, respect, and facilitators

A small company can implement a meeting system similar to ours if it has four or five employees. Larger businesses may have a different challenge: They may need to trim or reduce the number of unnecessary meetings. Caswell's meeting procedures can be invaluable for your organization. Regular weekly meetings don't need to be complex, bureaucratic events, but they all need some basics to work well:

1. **A regular schedule** – Set your meeting times at the same time each day or week to minimize operational disruption, and to make attendance as easy as possible. We settled on 1:30 p.m. Mondays for our general meetings and 3:00 on Thursdays for the sales meetings. The 1:30 start for the regular meeting allows everyone to participate, even employees on the West Coast. As a rule, afternoon meetings are much better for salespeople in our industry than morning sessions, because the most productive business and client contact is in the mornings. (Your situation may be different: For example, residential real estate representatives rarely meet clients on weekday mornings, so a morning meeting time may be better for your business.)

2. **Clear advance agenda, with minutes and action items** – Everyone receives an agenda before the meeting, and employees can add items for discussion. Attached to the agenda is an "action items" list with commitments by individual employees addressing objectives discussed in previous planning meetings.

3. **Clear rules and procedures** – Meetings always start on time and everyone agrees in advance not to accept phone calls. Those who must leave early, state this at the beginning. Meetings always start with a "deflation," an innocent question by one of the participants. This soft question allows us to confirm the speaking order, test phone link connections and the like, and settle into the serious agenda items without technical distractions. Sometimes the deflation questions and answers are entertaining and reveal personal details about meeting participants.

4. **Rotation of speaking order** – By establishing a speaking order, everyone is given a chance to participate and contribute. As well, we rotate the speaking order. For sales meetings, individual representatives take the lead in chairing each meeting. For the general meetings, as the chief executive officer, I lead the meeting unless I expect I may not be available. When that happens (rarely), I delegate the responsibility to a senior employee.

5. **Minutes and records** – An administrative employee takes minutes at each meeting. This note-taking allows everyone to focus on the meeting rather than recording it and the minutes are a useful record for those who cannot attend. The "action items" list is updated as well. This shows clear accountability for decisions taken during the meeting, and prevents ideas from falling off the radar screen.

Meetings don't need to be a burden

While we require employees to attend the regular meetings, consultants and independent contractors are not formally required to attend, but usually come when they are not engaged elsewhere. This is because the meetings allow them to connect quickly to the business rhythm, catch up on news, and share observations. Because the meetings rarely last the maximum one hour allocation, and we rarely schedule more than two meetings a week, meeting time takes up barely an hour every week. This is hardly a burden to anyone.

The daily huddle option

The daily huddle is a variation on the meeting concept, ideal for work groups concentrated in one location. Here, you bring everyone together for five or 10 minutes in the morning or near the end of the day. The huddle allows for quick discussion of current issues and work concerns. Businesses say it reduces time by quickly resolving issues in one session.

The annual planning meeting

The annual planning meeting (and in our case, the mid-year review) is a different kind of event. Everyone, even out-of-town employees, attends in person and we rely on our consultants to facilitate the event. These meetings tend to be costly since we need to pay for travel, accommodation, food and facilitator fees. As well, routine business operations including sales are deferred while we gather.

Our annual planning meetings last a full day, with a second day for a sales meeting and review. The mid-year review lasts about three to four hours with a special sales meeting in the afternoon.

Our goal is to frame the business plan and the macro-objectives, to look at the big picture, and to examine our progress. During informal sessions, employees and contractors who don't normally work together can share ideas and build more personal relationships.

Keeping on track

Of course, as the year progresses, plans can go off track. Sometimes employees want to implement new ideas or explore new business possibilities. Ideas proposed in the business plan may not evolve quite the way they should. These challenges are quickly resolved with our meeting system. We can adjust course at the weekly meetings and, for major decisions, modify strategies at the mid-year review.

The system is flexible. Last year, for example, a client proposed we engage in an entirely new business, outside the scope of our primary business plan. Knowing this enterprise could be useful, but also knowing it didn't fit into the existing plan, I set up another business with independent resources and its own plan, while informing employees of the new venture. (As well, we established a separate meeting system for participants in the additional business.) The result: Our company has a new profit centre without straining resources or relationships in the original business.

Do you need a consultant/facilitator?

I think most businesses require someone to facilitate the annual and bi-annual meetings. The individual should be an independent professional very familiar with your business. The challenge is to find the right person. Places to look include trade associations, friends in business, and clients or suppliers. They'll most likely welcome your call and you can build a short list of consultants and advisors. This also gives you an opportunity for follow up and connecting.

Avoiding the consulting traps

Here are some things for you to keep in mind in selecting your consultants:

The "big-name" consultants with published books and organized training programs can be good, but you will pay top dollar for their services and probably be referred to a junior employee within their organization. I would buy their written materials or DVDs and then call on a local professional who can help you implement the strategies.

You should have a clear idea about what you require and expect. This book offers you guidelines: Both a business plan and a meeting/communication system with employees are fundamental. Be wary of anything too complicated and open-ended; you could find yourself with an endless trail of invoices.

Once you have found someone in whom you have confidence, and who has proven to be effective, don't be afraid to pay for consulting services. Our company's meeting/planning budget is now in the range of $20,000 a year. This is not an insignificant sum, but it is worth every dollar. With the meetings and planning process, everyone pulls together and contributes to the success of the business.

Note: If your company is larger, with more than 20 employees, you may wish to break your planning process down by divisions and sections, which will appoint representatives to the overall planning committee. The model I'm using works well for businesses with five to 20 or so employees; if your company is smaller, wait until you have a few more employees. If you have a larger company, review your meeting/planning processes to avoid bureaucracy and top-down management.

The marketing plan and your overall business strategy

Smaller and mid-sized businesses do best building marketing and business development plans within the annual meeting/planning system. If your business is larger, say when your sales and marketing department have more than five or six employees, you may schedule a specialized annual marketing planning meeting, attended by senior executives who will then integrate the plans within the overall business planning process.

Make sure that your marketing-plan meeting involves those who must implement it most directly. Obviously your sales team as well as administrative and other project managers should be involved since they must live with its daily consequences.

You should align your marketing and sales meetings and individual planning sessions with the annual general meeting. At the general meeting, set your overall budget and goals. Put any significant expenses in your budget. Then should a sales representative or even a senior executive come up with an interesting proposal, you don't rush to change direction on a whim. As a team, you may choose to reallocate resources at the mid-year review or, if the matter is more urgent, at your weekly regular meetings.

The meeting system effectively builds discipline into your business decision-making processes. As new ideas come up during the year, you can adapt and include them. With everyone's participation, you avoid playing favourites or creating dissension behind the scenes.

Your marketing budget

How much should you spend on marketing? Probably the most rational budgeting system is to to assess and project your cost per sales lead, and the likely profitability of each lead. Of course, you will need some key numbers and metrics to design this type of budget, but I wouldn't be concerned about getting things 100 per cent right at first. Be very realistic and cautious in projecting future revenues from untried marketing techniques or media.

For example, you may need to spend thousands of dollars on some forms of advertising before you can even assess the results. If you are projecting revenues from an untried advertising/marketing strategy, make sure that you can live with the financial consequences if it is not as successful as you expect.

If you are looking for a rule-of-thumb marketing budget guideline, many contractors find a minimum of 5 per cent of gross sales is a good starting point. You may spend more – 10 per cent is often a reasonable number if you have many smaller accounts — depending on your business and resources. In a start-up situation, I would spend more of my 5 to 10 per cent on personal relationships, networking, and association/community activities than on conventional advertising. Established businesses should always give top priority to current and previous clients. If you are using business development or sales representatives, your budget will be higher. In this case, total sales and marketing costs may reach upwards of 25 per cent of sales. Obviously, if you are a "rainmaker" or have a partner/business associate generating business, the salary and incentive costs are part of the budget, often hidden in the compensation packages. If your marketing and sales budget is much greater than 25 per cent of revenue, you will have trouble delivering enough value to your clients at a fair price to maintain a sustainable business with a good brand/reputation. If you are spending less than 5 per cent, you are failing to cover the basics of marketing and business development, and are risking your business's ultimate viability. However, the actual numbers (and percentages) again will depend on many variables which you need to consider in your planning process.

Bottom up or top down management

Our company's system is founded on respecting the opinion of every individual in our organization. Sure, there is a boss, but everyone participates in the budget planning process, sees the numbers, and can see in the weekly review if we are on track. Involve all your employees in the meeting and planning processes, giving them the opportunity to participate and influence the course. With their participation and perceived ownership, your company will be able to withstand the storms, and take advantage of new opportunities.

Chapter 6
Your employees and your brand:
How to hire and retain the right people

How do you connect branding, marketing and business development into a cohesive strategy? If your business is in harmony, both internally and in its relationships with clients, the selling and marketing process is natural and spontaneous. Much of your new business will come through referred leads or bidding opportunities from repeat clients.

Since your employees and their relationships with each other and your clients are so important to the marketing process, it is crucial to have systems in place to find and retain the right employees, while encouraging those who don't fit in to leave quickly. This is especially important when considering the special class of employees responsible for finding new clients: your sales team and rainmakers.

What is a rainmaker?

Rainmakers combine professional expertise and knowledge with sales skills. They are the lifeblood of professional practices, particularly in the fields of architecture and engineering. Rainmakers are often business owners or founders, but any professional who is so inclined can become a rainmaker by learning how to combine selling and personal branding skills with their professional or technical knowledge and expertise.

The rainmaker's brand

Rainmakers and successful owners have the ability to create a personal brand that correlates to their business. In other words, they have the capacity to attract and build sufficient reputation and success that people choose to do business with them and their organization. Clearly, if a business or professional practice can attract and retain great rainmakers, it will grow a whole lot faster than if it can't. As well, it will be better positioned to survive any economic downturn.

Attracting and retaining rainmakers

The challenge is: How do you attract, train (if possible) and retain these precious individuals? You can either hope for the best or become pro-active. Business owners who wish to investigate the art of rain-making will certainly want to read Ford Harding's books on the topic or, if they have the resources, engage his consulting services. His book, *Creating Rainmakers: The Manager's Guide to Training Professionals to Attract New Clients*, is a must-read.

Harding explains that the process of finding and developing rain-making and sales talent within professional businesses and practices is not a simple thing. "They vary from professional to professional, and from firm to firm," he writes. "From all the possible ways to develop new business, each professional and firm must select a handful and make them work."

In other words, someone looking for a "one-size-fits-all" answer here, won't find it. You will get a lot closer, however, by looking at successful stories and adapting your own practices or the best ideas to your own business culture and operations.

Dedicated sales representatives

Relatively few architectural, engineering and contracting businesses employ sales representatives whose primary knowledge and ability is in sales. Perhaps this is because the stereotypical image of sales is so offensive that few technical professionals want to go in that direction. As well, your company may not need a sales representative to simply bid commodity-priced projects; you need a great estimator who is able to trim the fat on costs, finding the best prices and the lowest input expenses possible.

The other problem with conventional selling practices is they go against the grain of effective branding. I don't know of many people who want to be sold anything; so when confronted with a pushy sales rep, unless the representative is really good, they will push back and resist.

Rainmaking rewards justify the risks

Nevertheless, if you have the choice of hiring a really strong sales representative or rainmaker for $100,000 or spending the same money on advertising, you will want to make sure that you recruit and hire the right representative.

Are your estimators your marketers?

Many contractors and those in the subtrades believe that their marketing process begins and ends with the work of their estimators. Undoubtedly, good estimating skills are vital for success in this business; you need to know your true costs and also the most efficient and economical way to carry out your projects. However, success in marketing is less tied to lowest cost than the ability to help clients achieve the most successful results. An instance of effective estimating combined with marketing is when you can suggest to clients, both before and after you win the contract, cost-saving improvements that won't interfere with (but may even help) the project's functionality.

In other words, your estimators will be successful not just because they can deliver the lowest "bid" on time, but because they can show clients that you always have their best interests in mind.

Sales training and resources

Experts in rainmaking are few and far between. Harding is the best I know, but many books, training programs and systems have been developed for selecting and training sales people. You will certainly gain some value from these resources, however, in my opinion, they really only work when they correlate with your brand and marketing success.

If your company's brand and relationship-building approaches are successful, you'll find it much easier to attract the right rainmakers and sales reps. You'll also find they need not push nearly as hard to find and develop profitable business.

Take, for example, sales trainer and marketing guru Jeffrey Gitomer, who attracts thousands to his sales training seminars and programs around the world. Gitomer says, sure, cold calling is effective. He then demonstrates by making a cold call himself. Calling the same person a struggling sales rep is trying to meet, Gitomer identifies himself and quickly gets through. Why? Gitomer has achieved enough fame within the sales and business communities that he's a celebrity in his own right. You too would most likely return a call from the leading public figure in your marketing space.

Great branding makes selling easy

Simply put, if your branding – either as a business, organization or individual – is truly successful, your selling job will be easy. Potential clients will be predisposed to trust you, to accept your cold calls, to put you on the RFP short list (and then finalist list) and, even better, to wire the competition so you are virtually sure to win. You can achieve that success by delivering the goods, learning the skills involved, and enhancing the entire client/marketing experience.

Natural talent or learned ability

Can you learn how to be a great sales representative? You certainly can if you have the will, drive, and certain natural personality traits. I've already explained that you achieve the best results in anything you do by harnessing your strengths rather than forcing yourself to be someone you are not.

Rainmakers or marketing?

Should you select and hire only great salespeople and rainmakers, and not worry about marketing? This is a good question. One could argue (see above) that if your marketing department and processes are really good and totally integrated within your overall business practices, anyone can sell, without working very hard at it. But most businesses and professional practices still need at least one person with the sense about where to go and find new business. In the early going, the owner or founders have this role. After all, they grew the business or professional practice from scratch. Often these owner-founded businesses or professional practices have great trouble transitioning to the next generation, unless they find a way to develop and train the right rainmaking sales team.

An alternative approach is to build a systematic yet flexible hiring process for sales and marketing talent. As well, the business owner can extrapolate this approach to ALL hiring processes. If you are careful about how you select employees and consultants you will likely be successful in hiring decisions. If you play by the seat of your pants, you may be lucky or have exceptionally good intuition, but you will encounter many problems and stresses along the way.

How to find and recruit rainmakers and sales representatives

Culled from many books on the topic and many of my own mistakes, following are strategies I've found to be most effective in finding and keeping an excellent sales team:

1. **Create a business environment so emotionally satisfying and rewarding that great employees will want to work for the organization and stay.** In addition, provide a path to ownership or partnership for as many employees who want to follow that route as possible.

2. **Concentrate on real work achievements rather than resumes and interviews.** Resumes can be dressed up, and interviews structured so that a less-than-perfect candidate looks great. Sometimes even references are set up and coached. Our approach is to ask all candidates on our short list to work with us for a brief period. We then learn if they are able to do the job and can get along well with their colleagues. It is a much more effective approach than subjecting the candidates to multiple interviews, or worse, hiring a "bad fit" who is skilled at doing interviews.

3. **Use a pre-screening employee questionnaire.** You can customize questions to assess the prospective employee's competence, interest in the work, and set the stage for proper reference checking and work skills evaluation. Best of all, the questionnaire puts you in the driver's seat. You control the format and style, and thus can look beyond "resume-speak" in your assessments. The questionnaire also serves as a really effective screening tool: You are looking for someone who will put a little effort in responding.

4. **In some cases, use personality tests and evaluation tools.** We've found Salestestonline.com offers the best and most effective screening resource for our company: The test is fast, inexpensive, and surprisingly valid. By comparison, other tests are costly and relatively complex to administer. Additionally, for good salespeople, they are annoying to complete.

Beware of assumptions and prejudices

First impressions are important, but these should be measured and validated by performance, not appearance. I recall my introduction to a great sales representative who was working with us on a major joint venture project. "This guy is old, washed up, and I don't know where (my joint venture partner) found him," I thought. Then he reported his early and astoundingly successful sales results.

He shared his personal history when we finally sat down for dinner at a trade association meeting. "Years ago, I worked as an estimator/representative for a printing company," he said. "There was an aluminum casting business I wanted to sell some printing services to, but the company president wouldn't return my calls. So one day I got up early, drove to the plant, and parked in the company president's parking spot.

"When the president showed up, I told him: 'I'll give your space back if you give me 20 minutes of your time.'" The president did, and and my friend sold him a complex and profitable brochure design and printing project, which entailed several months of work.

After completing the job and delivering the product, my sales friend received a call from the company president, saying he would like to meet with him.

So he showed up at the plant and the president offered him a job with the company. "The benefits, salary and opportunity were too good to pass up," the salesman recalled. Subsequently, the salesperson went to work there, changing standard practices, leading an invigorated team, helping to build the company into a multi-million dollar international organization. By the time he retired, he had achieved independent wealth.

Typical of high achievers, he became bored with a traditional retirement. So he launched a new career working with our joint venture partner.

Capturing your opportunities

The aluminum casting company president had the insight to recognize talent. He could see that the salesperson not only used creativity to get his foot in the door, he also delivered the goods. The president didn't need sales tests and resumes to evaluate this type of ability.

The dangers of relying on one superstar

Relying too much on one sales superstar is one of the biggest risks and dangers in any business. If you founded the business, this person could be you or someone you hired. Really effective rainmakers and sales representatives can be so effective that they alienate everyone else in your organization, or even more dangerously, sell to their personal objectives at the expense of your brand. As well, if they account for most of your sales, their leaving would put you under immense pressure and threaten the company's viability.

I know of a top sales representative who worked primarily on the phone, but could sell more in a few hours than others who struggled for a month. She worked on pure commission and knew her power. However, she ultimately alienated key people in our niche community by high pressure sales, by going behind people's backs, and by putting her sales agenda first and foremost in any communications with customers.

We depended on her for virtually all of our business, so how could we ask her to leave?

Ultimately, as our business reached a low point, circumstances led to her resignation. This turned out to be a blessing in disguise when I realized we could offer a base salary to a new sales rep based on established contract ad sales. Using our hiring system, we found some competent sales reps right away. This is a powerful lesson: A bad employee can poison your business culture and destroy your brand.

The solutions: Excellent communications and solid employment contracts

A regular company meeting system, as described in the previous chapter, is the best control on any employee threatening your business and brand through self-interest. You can quickly capture and resolve inconsistencies or problems. Effective communications will go a long way toward preventing soured relationships and turf wars.

Also essential are solid employment contracts. Working with a qualified employment lawyer, take the time to draft legally correct employment contracts. Ensuring that contracts and employment practices comply with local laws and regulations will keep you out of trouble. Beware: You can dig yourself into a really big legal hole if you are ignorant of the laws and processes of terminating employees you want to leave. It is far better to head off trouble by combining an effective contract with solid employee communications. Troublesome employees will often resign of their own accord, without your having to pay them severance.

Technical and non-sales employees

The principles in this chapter apply to hiring all employees, not just sales and marketing specialists. Look first for employees with natural ability in their area of interest. Then look for a strong co-operative spirit to ensure that they will work well with others in the organization. We always ask prospective employees to demonstrate their skills in a trial assignment. We also encourage them to attend our weekly meeting and spend some time with current employees. We then evaluate their successes in the trial project, considering their technical skills and their fit within the company culture.

Learn your lessons

If you take the time to develop skills to evaluate and select rainmakers and business development specialists, you can then apply the same principles for all employee hiring. By hiring correctly, you will create a thriving working environment, which your current and potential clients will notice when they are considering whether to work with your business. The combination of enthusiastic employees working together and a great brand reputation will bring your strengths forward in the marketplace, and you will win all around.

Chapter 7
Do what you do well and enjoy it

Your marketing success closely relates to this simple principle:

Everyone in your organization combines an enthusiasm for their work, respect for peers, and passion and satisfaction in being the best at who they are.

As an individual: "Do what you do well and enjoy it."
As a company: "Work together in harmony, using your abilities and interests, while respecting the needs of your clients and fellow employees."

Corporate lip service or real harmony?

You can quantify and measure your success, but when the measuring process becomes an end in itself, you fall into a major trap. Similarly, if you only pay lip-service to these concepts, while forcing them into a corporate policy manual and structured management processes, you will not achieve your desired effect. Everyone might wear false smiles when what they really want to do is trash their computers.

So how do you achieve a natural harmony that becomes part of the everyday culture of your organization?

Structured meetings bring people together

The structured meetings I described earlier are part of the answer. These processes do bring everyone together. Some work groups effectively combine the weekly, or brief twice-weekly meetings with five-minute daily huddles, usually standing, either at the beginning or the end of the work day. In addition, they schedule all day planning and review sessions once or twice a year, plus quarterly or bi-annual social gatherings that help loosen any interpersonal tensions.

Accountability and power: Your employees have authority

The freedom and courage to be yourself is another important ingredient for success. If you are an owner or manager, you must allow your employees to be accountable for themselves. This includes having the authority and power to take decisions in their day-to-day work and with clients. In other words, employees need enough authority that they can solve client problems on the spot or can commit company resources to deal with them.

This also means you need to have trust in yourself, your peers and employees. When trust is reciprocated, you achieve a company with internal harmony, an environment in which good clients are eager to do business and will pay the prices required for your profitability.

Trimming the rules

Look at your company rule books, policy manuals, and processes to see if you can eliminate at least 20 per cent of them: Rules and systems set up to accommodate circumstances long-since passed, meetings held for reasons no longer valid, and so on. Then, once you've knocked off 20 per cent, go for the next. It may be extreme to suggest that you can remove 80 per cent of your rules and have a viable, well-run business. The idea is to trim down the bureaucracy and yet have enough control for freedom to take action. I would never suggest taking such drastic measures in one step or without legal guidance where necessary, but you may be surprised how far you can go to simplify things.

Some simple guidelines

Then follow some simple guidelines that will become your ongoing practices. For example, consider "Pooles Rules" from PCL Construction founder Ernest Poole, which form the basis of the employee-owned general contractor's success in multi-million dollar annual volume.

- Employ highest grade people obtainable.
- Encourage integrity, loyalty and efficiencies.
- Avoid side lines.
- Do not permit side lines by employees.
- Be fair in all dealings with owners, architects, engineers and subcontractors.
- Keep your word as good as your bond.
- Give encouragement and show appreciation.

- Be firm, fair and friendly.
- Avoid jobs where design is not good or financing doubtful. Let your competitors have these.
- Maintain good accounting and cash keeping. They are essential.
- Do not let finishing up of jobs or collecting payments lag.

How to engage your employees in the business:

1. Engage all employees in setting the budget and business plan.

Invite all employees to contribute to the setting of the company's budget and business plan. Everyone can participate directly in the full-scale final planning meeting until you grow past 12 to 15 employees; then you may need to set separate divisional or functional planning meetings where employees contribute their input, and delegate a representative to attend the final, formal meeting.

2. Give all employees the freedom to improvise (within guidelines) in adapting the budget and business plan.

Throughout the year, with a business plan and processes, any employee may propose and present an idea they think may work. If it is "off plan" the idea can be tabled until the planning meeting, or the idea can be modified to work within the plan.

To give a recent example from our company:

One of our sales reps received a proposal from a construction association in his service area to produce a magazine.

"We are fed up with the high pressure sales techniques of the previous magazine publisher, and we would like you to do the work," the Association Manager told our employee. This inquiry was a sure sign we had achieved branding and marketing success, but we publish newspapers, not magazines. In our business model, magazines are expensive to produce, and our operating systems were not been set up to accommodate magazine publishing.

Our sales rep could have said, "Sure, let's do it." A quick thinker, he suggested instead, "Why don't we produce a special quarterly supplement to our newspaper for you?" The association executive readily agreed.

In another instance, one of our representatives was approached by general trade associations to produce annual printed business directories. We discussed the idea at our annual planning meeting, and as a result, we have expanded our product line to produce these directories.

3. Employee contracts

In our company, all employees must sign a contract when joining the organization. The contract describes major policies including provisions for termination, compensation levels and expense reimbursement limits. Thus the rules are clearly laid out to avoid contentious issues.

Throwing the rule book away

With planning and policies in the foreground and the employee contract in the background, our company culture is not dominated by a rigid set of rules. For example, here is our travel policy regarding personal expenses:

"Do what is reasonable."

Travel of course is one area of business practice where controls and abuse are common. Our control is to have one key employee as travel co-ordinator, with the responsibility for booking travel and reviewing employee travel plans. At the same time, this co-ordinator doesn't overrule individual employees who have the authority to circumvent the rules because of specific circumstances.

"Different employees have different needs, and forcing everyone in a corporate straightjacket of policy guidelines will tear away at the individual's ability to take responsibility for their own choices," our travel co-ordinator explains.

"We've had situations where employees have stayed in flea-bag hotels to save money, but compensated with a splurge at a fancy restaurant. This isn't a problem."

Freedom, responsibility and accountability

When employees are free to be themselves, yet still accountable, you gain the best of all worlds. Your employees look forward to each day's work, and they pitch in when there are problems. Most importantly, they connect with your clients in such an effective manner that your brand recognition and acceptance reach the highest level, and, yes, people start calling you and inviting you to do work without even wanting the competition anywhere nearby.

Then, and here is the fun part, combining some simple measuring and management resources with this freedom, you can plan for growth, set and achieve your marketing objectives, and build a thriving business in good times and hard.

Recapturing your passion by being who you are

Wake up each morning committed to being your best at what you enjoy the most, and encourage your employees, peers and clients to share the same attitudes and freedoms. Put your policy guidelines away, have fun, and look forward to your day's challenges. This is not to advocate carelessness, "anything goes" management. It is a call for you to respect yourself, your employees and your clients.

Have fun. Do what you love doing. Allow your peers and employees the same freedom within reasonable guidelines. Your service standards will soar; your clients (and potential clients) will connect with you and your brand power. Profitability will reach the highest levels. Done right, marketing will almost seem effortless within your overall business culture and practices. Your phone will ring, your email will ping, and either a colleague or client will whisper into your ear an advance tip on a project or business opportunity with the next words: "We would like you to do the job."

When that happens on a regular and measurable basis, you'll know you've succeeded – and achieved success in marketing your company.

Now, it is time to look at some specific suggestions and techniques you may apply to your own business.

When sales representatives play to your emotions . . .

It's important to keep your eyes open to what your clients really want. At the same time, beware of marketing media and sales reps tailoring their products and services to suit your emotions rather than your current and prospective clients.

For example, you might enjoy listening to the high-brow news or public radio station, while your clients are interested in top 40 hits. Should you advertise on the high-brow station because you like it? The sales rep from the hard-rock station senses your love of sports and gives you a couple of prized tickets to an NFL game. Do you buy from this person because of his generosity? These risks are magnified when you delegate authority for major marketing purchases to employees outside the framework of a business plan, as they may be tempted to take the offers, thus swaying their business decisions.

Here is a simple strategy to avoid the risks of buying marketing services you like, rather than those you need.

Spend your time on tasks and projects doing what you love. Spend your money on activities you don't want to do yourself, but always be guided by your plan, strategy and business objectives.

For example, by having a clearly defined and thought-through budget for major expenses, you are less likely to allow media sales representatives to sway your decisions. You will know your goals and market priorities, and you will allocate funds where they can truly provide you with the highest value.

Having fun and enjoying your work – and encouraging these attitudes among your staff – doesn't mean careless expenditures on marketing that satisfies your interests but not those of your clients. Use common sense. You may indeed discover that season's tickets for your favourite sporting events are a wise (and fun) business expense. Engage in marketing activities that not only capture your passions, but are also relevant to your clients' interests and values.

Construction Marketing Ideas

**Practical strategies and resources to attract
and retain profitable clients for your architectural,
engineering or construction business**

PART II

Practical marketing observations and suggestions

Chapter 1

How to take control of your marketing

You know by now that most of your construction marketing success will be achieved through your overall business values and your company's passion for enjoying and achieving the highest quality work and client relationships. With a solid brand built through your healthy business practices, current clients will return and will refer their friends and colleagues.

However, passively relying on referrals and repeat clients is risky business. Just as the 80/20 (or, more accurately, 76/24 rule) suggests that most of your new business will arise from repeat and referral sources, you run serious business risks when you fall into the trap of allowing 75 to 80 per cent of your business to come from one or two good clients. Too many times I've heard the sad story of otherwise well-run, reputable, and efficient businesses collapsing when their best clients fail. When you put all of your eggs into one or two baskets, you know what happens when the baskets break.

Similarly, passively relying on repeat and referral business can cause you real grief if, for any reason, things slow down, such as in a recession. Will you then resort to drastic (and usually dumb) measures such as blind price cutting, desperate and ill-thought advertising, or thoughtlessly answering every bidding or RFP announcement, even though with just a little review, you could see that the proposed projects are already wired in favour of others, or would be totally unprofitable for you if you win them?

Select the approaches right for your business

Fortunately, you can take control of your marketing with planned approaches to network effectively, to develop new leads, to encourage repeat and referral business. Additionally it is important to know when and how to use the other techniques and resources including advertising, leads services, cold canvassing (in some cases) and telemarketing.

Be thoughtful about which methodologies in this section you use. You want to be sure they are compatible with your values, your business culture, and the actual business you deliver. You also will want to be sure that they are right for your employees. Everyone is different. You may find some of your employees actually enjoy (and are great) at canvassing, while others can design and take pictures for great RFP presentations (and in some cases, multi-task, turning a planned "keep in touch" call to gather images for the next RFP into an opportunity to seek repeat business or direct, informal referrals.)

Specific methods to increase your marketing effectiveness

In the pages ahead, you will learn about specific methods to measurably increase your repeat and referral business (while attracting new clients) including follow-up visits and letters, referral incentives, and media publicity. You will then read about my favourite marketing resource, trade and community associations, and how you can turn strategic association membership and participation into both short and impressive long-term gains. You'll learn about the most effective approaches to networking, media publicity, advertising (print and on line), canvassing and leads services. I will also explore on-line resources including blogs, search engine placement, and paid Internet advertising.

In a special section, you will read about how to work with and use salespeople to find business — whether they are rainmakers (professional services) or inexpensive telemarketers — and which approaches work best, including our effective training of sales reps to think as marketers more than salespeople, applying in practice "sarketing" principles.

As you read these pages, take notes about which approaches will be best for your business, and then validate them with your own network and employees before rushing into action. Most importantly, be wary of outside salespeople calling on you to encourage you to engage in one activity or another, and look closely at anything you've been doing over time to make sure it still works today. You'll be able to resolve your choices within a planned strategy that will give you security and control over your marketing, whether times are good or challenging.

How to ask for referrals

Sure, you enjoy the experience, when out of the seeming blue, people call or email you and invite you to do business with them. Often they volunteer the source: They had heard you are good from one of your current or previous clients, or they recall doing business with you in the past and are happy to give you some further work.

How often (and how do you) ask your current and previous clients to do business with you again? Sometimes, perhaps more often than you wish, you find this process uncomfortable, seemingly beneath your dignity. You are afraid of rejection, perhaps, or more importantly, of putting a negative selling cloud on your warm current client relationships.

However, I know of no more effective and rapid-response business development technique than to ask your current and former clients for new business or referrals. You can and should set the processes for this type of asking as your most significant and immediate business development resource.

Inviting referrals and repeat business: The best immediate marketing solution

Your ability to ask for new business and referrals may in fact save your business in hard times as things start drying up. You may find your current and former clients dig into their memories or find a modest job that needs to be done now, and they provide you the work out of respect.

Some sales pundits suggest scripted, structured and formalized processes to dig out referrals, and I agree with these approaches, to a point. Improvements in your techniques in asking for and seeking out repeat and referral business will pay back far more than any other form of marketing I know. You don't need to be a pest about it, and you don't need to force the issue.

Here are some suggestions on how to set the stage to ask for referrals and repeat business:

Your built-in follow-up service call

The late Sonny Lykos advocates this strategy, and it makes sense on more than one level. He says when you contract with clients, include a budget for free follow- and fix-up inspection and service following completion of your project. The number and frequency of these calls of course depends on the project, its complexity, and your client relationships, but you can build these into your initial contract as part of your warranty/follow-up service commitments.

When you complete the follow-up service calls, you are in a natural place to meet, relate and communicate with your clients, and you can always (easily) ask if there is more work that needs to be done, perhaps pointing out something worthy of attention. You can also simply ask for referrals.

The bonus service call

A variation of the pre-planned service call (set up at the time you initially begin relationship) is an approach successfully used by builder/renovator Hopkins and Porter in Potomac, MD. The company, on its 25th anniversary, sent a letter to approximately 2,000 former clients offering a free hour's handyman services in exchange for permission to install a lawn sign. Marketing consultant Jon Goldman says the company achieved a 32 per cent response rate and $375,000 in sales. "Every business has an anniversary; it could be five years, three years, even one year, and this would work," says Goldman.

Asking with your thank you cards

Hand-written thank you notes are powerful marketing resources. Few businesses effectively use them, and when you receive this type of personalized communication, most of the time you have a warm and respectful feeling for the experience. (Reflecting this fact, our business policy is that all advertising representatives send a personal thank you note whenever they receive new business.)

Marketing consultant David Frey suggests appending a note to your individually-written thank you cards:

"I learned this tactic, strangely enough, by Princess Diana and a local real estate agent. When Princess Diana died a close associate of hers was interviewed and revealed that Diana always carried a set of "royal" thank you notes.

"Every time she met with someone she would remember their names and as soon as she got in her car she would write a short thank you note to them. The people cherished the thank you notes they received from the Princess. After hearing that, I started to carry around my own box of thank you notes.

"But here's what really will make this referral tactic take off. Not long ago I received an email from a subscriber to my *Marketing Best Practices Newsletter* that had this phrase under the man's signature:

> **By Referral Only**
>   *By Referral Only...means: We invest 100 per cent of our time and energy to delivering first-class service to our clients. As a result, our valued clients, suppliers, and friends refer their family, friends and work associates to us for advice on buying or selling real estate. We're interested in building strong life long relationships one person at a time.*

"You see, its not enough to send a thank you note. People need to know that you want and appreciate their referrals. The phrase, in essence, answers the question, "What can you do for me in return for this nice thank you card?" Immediately, I had this phrase printed on the bottom of my thank you notes and my referrals took off."

Specific or general

Sometimes it is helpful, in requesting referrals, to prime the pump with a few additional questions. Just asking "Do you know anyone else who could use my services?" might result in a blank stare, or, "I'll think it over." More effective, by far, would be your asking your clients about the associations and community groups that they support, and then (once you know what they are) determining whether you want to support or participate in the groups (see the chapter on association marketing for more insights here). If you provide a regionalized residential or commercial service, you could ask the person for insights into their neighbours' needs and interests, again inviting referrals.

Suppliers and clients

Your own business's suppliers and clients may become your best source of referrals, and you can adapt the supply chain into a powerful ongoing source of new and repeat business. This has become our most lucrative business source as we build our advertising sales through supplier-supported advertising features.

Here's why. You are giving business/money to these companies, and they in return will be happy to return the favour, if you ask.

In fact, some businesses build most of their client base through this form of referral. Your suppliers are not likely to be offended if you call them and ask the referral-seeking question: After all, you are their client, and they (if they are any good) will want to treat you well.

I learned the power of supplier-chain referrals through the late Walt Haily's *Breaking the No Barrier* and it is our single most effective (and valid) way to sell advertising to construction businesses. When we invite owners and general contractors to send letters, faxes or emails to their suppliers asking them to advertise in our publications, our sales representatives don't have to work too hard to obtain orders. (Of course we are careful not to abuse the trust and relationships here; we will deliver genuine value to every advertiser and treat our clients with the same level of respect they treat theirs.)

Some businesses live completely from supplier referrals. This is an easy way to find business, but risky if you are relying on one or two suppliers for most of your referrals: You don't want to ever be dependent on a single source of business, in case relationships sour or your referring business fails. You are simply handing too much power over your destiny to another organization.

Peer group referrals

You may find value in participating in organized business exchange and referral groups. These are special business associations such as Business Networking International (BNI) or the International Executives' Association, where non-competing businesses get together at local chapters/meetings on a regular schedule to exchange news and business leads and referrals. "An Executives Association is an elite business networking organization founded for one purpose: to share confidential business leads and information among its Member Firms," the IEA website says.

If you wish to take a leadership role, you may find you can develop your own peer networking, lead exchange or "masterminding" group. This takes more work and effort, of course, but you magnify its power for your business because of your leadership initiative.

Should you pay for referrals?

Some businesses systematically offer compensation to current and former clients (and sometimes outsiders) for referrals, perhaps paying as much as they would a commercial leads service for the information that is the same or similar but obviously of much greater value. You can create special referral cards for clients to share with friends and associates: When you receive a referral that converts to business, send the agreed-on money or gift. You may discover a few true bird-dogs who generate thousands of dollars of business for you each year.

This type of referral can be linked to community and association participation. For example, as a contractor, you offer to contribute $200 per successful referral to members of local church or sports organizations of which you are a member.

Some businesses such as Feazel Roofing in Columbus, Ohio, adapt this model with a two-part compensation plan: They invite referrals by offering $50 to the referring person, and granting a $50 discount to the person they refer. Most creatively, Feazel Roofing allows the referrers to sign over their $50 to their friends – creating a $100 service saving (and of course saving Feazel Roofing any cash cost from the referral.)

Business-to-business referral compensation

Bobby Darnell of Construction Marketing Consultants in Atlanta, Georgia says that, in seven years of business, he has obtained about 10 per cent of his business volume through finders fee referrals. He offers a sliding scale of incentives, based on (1) the amount of work you do to provide the lead and the strength of the direct referral and (2) the value of the business you help generate for him.

He has granted me permission to make his lead finding system available, which you can download at the *Construction Marketing Ideas* blog site (go to the Darnell Referrals link at www.constructionmarketingideas.com).

Darnell says most people using his lead rewards program have contributed a single lead. The only potential conflict he had occurred when someone submitted a lead for a contact with whom Darnell had already been working. In this case, he simply provided documentation proving the prior relationship.

Referral centres of influence

Your most powerful referrals come from special people with high networking and connecting power. I'll cover networking techniques later, but for this chapter, consider people in your community who know and influence many others; they can be formal leaders or informal community organizers (whose prominence, either positive or negative, has risen in the United States). If you successfully conduct business or win the support of these powerful people, your referral volume will skyrocket.

Always acknowledge and respect your referral providers

Keep in touch. Send personal thank you notes. Even if you don't offer cash compensation (which often is unnecessary or may be offensive to the person providing the referrals), they will always appreciate the courtesy of communication and attention. I advocate making your connection as personal and "connected" as possible, and to respect the frequency of communication they wish.

Measuring your results

Obviously, if you use a system of referral cards or forms, you will have a tracking resource. But you should implement a simple recording system to keep track of (a) where your referrals are originating, (b) the value and nature of the referral and (c) your follow up communications with referral sources. Then you can input your total revenue and possibly profit per transaction, and with this information captured, use it to set targets and develop business projections. Initially, you'll need some discipline to capture the information. Probably your early efforts will be less-than-effective, especially as you determine the most consistent and effective measuring tool. (Then you have to go back to the drawing board and reset your measurements.) The reason you won't rush to measure is that the immediate value will seem vague. For most businesses, especially contractors and professional services with a long business/sales cycle, you will need upwards of a year or two to capture everything you need to know. However, with enough time you then can plug in the variables into your business plan and set specific targets and objectives moving forward.

Why bother systematizing the referral process?

You may say: "I get enough business through referrals without doing anything special to encourage more – sometimes I ask, but most of the time, people just call me." The danger here is that you are giving up control of your business destiny to unseen and (unless you manage them) uncontrollable sources.

Consultant Michael Stone expresses concern when he sees businesses relying on this type of referral business. "Our clients tell us that referrals have dried up to the point that they are almost non-existent," he says, advocating that construction businesses find at least six sources of leads, largely through advertising.

Stone is right, to a point. Far too many contractors simply rely on referrals and repeat clients. With their strong reputation for service and value (and thus an excellent brand), they in good times don't need to do anything to make the phone ring. In fact, they have a backlog of work, and it seems any assertive marketing would just overload their systems and result in less-than-satisfactory service.

Referrals: Capturing the low-hanging fruit

If your quality/service brand is good enough that you achieve this type of natural business in good times, you will find when things slow down that your highest and most successful return on marketing investment is to focus on your existing and previous clients. The referral-seeking tools outlined here will provide the best results, in the quickest time. They are similar to picking the low-hanging fruit in the orchard. You might not be able to rely on them for all of your business, especially if you wish to grow rapidly or you need to sustain your operations through a prolonged business downturn or recession. However, they will undoubtedly provide the most effective return on your marketing investment, in terms of both cost and time for response.

Simply put, before you use any of the other marketing methods suggested in this book, review and study this chapter, and plan your strategies to systematically improve and enhance your referral and repeat business. Then measure your results. You will be impressed by the profits you achieve.

Chapter 2

Association marketing:
Your untapped gold mine

After attending a Society for Marketing Professional Services (SMPS) annual Build Business convention in Denver, Colorado, our family visited a small working gold mine. The miner, after years of low gold prices, had discovered a way to survive by selling site visits to tourists. With gold prices soaring, the actual mining operation is now thriving. Nevertheless, the tourist revenue continues to create an exceptionally profitable business, and the miner doesn't need to dress the place up as a tourist site; it is a working mine, after all.

Discovering untapped resources

From a marketing perspective, associations have similarities to the gold mine. They can seem expensive, and while you can sometimes find nuggets on the surface, the best value is deep within your participation. However, unlike the mine, which (even if it can continue for decades) is a depleting resource, effective association participation results in increasing advantages until you hit the motherload of consistent, repeating opportunities.

It took me a long time to appreciate why associations are so valuable for marketing, and my research suggests that many people give up before they achieve success. A senior SMPS member said the association struggles with people who join, then quit after a year or two. "This turnover is disturbing, because the real value in membership comes with time and the networking and leads developed over the years," he said.

Patient membership permits long-term benefits

For example, early in my business (established in 1988), I joined the Greater Ottawa Home Builders' Association (GOHBA), thinking that membership might be helpful in developing leads for my regional real estate and construction publications.

I attended the regular dinner meetings, paying the meal fees on top of the heavy dues. As the early 1990s recession began, I thought about cancelling my membership, but I decided to hold on for another year.

Then, I received a fateful call. "We would like you to quote on producing a new newsletter for our association," the marketing director of the city's largest real estate developer told me. (It turned out he initiated the call after a fellow board member, a major building supply dealer and one of my earliest advertisers, suggested the idea at an association board meeting.)

I asked, "How much competition will I have?" The association director responded, "None. You are the only member in the category."

We set out to produce *The Impact!*, which has continued for 18 years, our longest-running publication The enterprise has resulted in significant spin-off business, including other association newsletters, a major renovation publication joint venture, and thousands of dollars in sales for our other publications.

Your highest marketing priority

With this experience, and others over the years, I've elevated association participation to the highest marketing priority. Our business doesn't pay for advertising (we sometimes trade with non-competing media), but we spend thousands of dollars each year on association dues, meetings and conventions. Over time, we've learned some basic principles which will help you to gain more value from your membership and reduce the cash drain.

Two association classes

You can choose to belong to two association classes. The first represents your industry or trade, and members are largely your peers and often competitors. The second represents the interests of the industry, trade, or community of your current and potential clients – your market. In some cases – in ours, it is the Society for Marketing Professional Services – a single association represents both groups.

You should give priority to client-focussed associations. For example, if you are a general contractor building hospitals and schools, your real marketing power occurs when you join relevant school and hospital facilities management and capital planning groups. While I believe there are many reasons to participate in your own trade groups (including knowledge exchange, inter-city referrals, and competitive intelligence gathering), if your budgets are limited, join client-oriented associations first.

Your current clients can guide you

Your current clients can tell you which associations are most valuable to them. Which groups do they support? Are they on the board of directors or executive? Most associations have a supplier/affiliate/supporter category where you will be welcomed.

Ask your clients if you can join them as a guest at one of their association events and see if they will introduce you or nominate you for membership. You might offer to pay for the golf game or social event, but often the association will absorb the costs in its search for new members.

The more expensive, the better

I've discovered the most effective associations have the highest dues. If you only pay $100 to $200 a year, you will find limited support and resources. You will meet many salespeople and small business owners, rather than senior representatives of companies with meaningful opportunities. (This observation applies to business groups. If you work with the general public, you will find community, church and fraternal groups have relatively low dues but may still be truly effective for your marketing.)

The more specialized, the better

Clearly, if you belong to a small community, your Chamber of Commerce may be ideal. In larger communities, you should belong to associations relevant to your specific focus and niche. Generalist associations usually cover too wide a swath to allow you to develop relationships relevant to your business.

Going beneath the surface – digging deeper

Associations are like most communities. If you have left your home town to move to another city, you may have noticed that initially you receive a warm reception, but then things get a little lonely. Without local connections, you may feel you don't really belong – and pushing too hard makes things worse.

Unless your current clients are members and you have a ready-made network to start, you will wonder why you are paying the dues only to encounter representatives selling insurance, association journal advertising, or expensive convention fees.

You need to patiently build your relationships.

The counterintuitive opportunity

If you are looking for quid-pro-quo return on investment, you are likely to be disappointed. You will be giving, giving, giving, and nothing will be returned, at least at the start. When you join (unless you have client contacts to smooth the way), you are an outsider, and it looks like you will stay that way, forever.

In the next chapter, I'll show you how to overcome these problems. First, however, you need to measure your association membership value differently. Put away the balance sheet and focus on sharing. You need to patiently and without any expectation of return share your time, ideas, and initiatives to support the associations' interests.

Choose your associations carefully

Because successful association marketing takes time and energy, you'll find you can only focus on a few groups. (If your business is larger or operates in several cities, you can allocate your marketing budget to memberships for local sales representatives or regional managers). You will gain the best results with:

- Associations with a strong membership referral credo: This is more common within the Home Builders Associations than the general or mixed construction groups, but there are exceptions;
- Associations where at least a few of your current clients are members, and where you can see other potential clients supporting and participating in the group;
- Associations supporting activities you enjoy: You'll be more likely to contribute and stay the course if you are having fun.

The real association membership value will occur when you start thinking creatively outside the guidelines of the conventional orientation process. Be patient. In time, you will discover the marketing gold mine within the associations you support.

Chapter 3

Associations (part 2):
Have fun, doing what you do best

You will succeed with associations by planning your participation carefully to align with your interests and values. Have fun and contribute where you have the strongest skills.

Don't worry about immediate marketing results. You will be successful with a long-term perspective.

Association committees are usually open to any member wishing to participate, and your ideas and initiatives will almost always be accepted.

Control your participation to do what you really like

Don't say, "I'll do anything." If you do, association staff or senior members may encourage you to participate on a committee or project far from your interests and marketing objectives. They are looking for warm bodies to help on tasks which few enjoy.

If you enjoy the tasks others don't like – especially in canvassing or selling memberships or services – you will be a hero. However, you should focus on activities that you enjoy and for which you have talent. You should look forward with enthusiasm and anticipation to your association participation.

Associations allow you to make your own choices and selections. If you enjoy writing, you can contribute to the association newsletter; if you like parties and social activities, you can join in the event planning committee and co-ordinate sporting or golf events. You can suggest ideas that appeal to you, and most likely your proposal will be accepted if you are enthusiastic about it.

Go with the flow but don't worry about immediate results

You can make virtually all the mistakes in the world and still have a second or third chance. As a volunteer, you can't be fired or demoted, so you don't need to worry about taking risks and trying out new ideas. Of course, you don't want to bang your head against the wall with failure or alienate your association colleagues. Still, you should not be afraid to experiment and discover your hidden talents.

Spend time more than money

When you join the association, you will receive many invitations to spend money. You will be invited to advertise in the association directory, sponsor events, and sign up for training programs and courses. Stand back, and think carefully about the these services' true marketing value.

I would go slow at first. As a secondary sponsor, you'll likely achieve limited if any direct marketing results, and when your cash is depleted with no measurable benefit, you'll likely approach your third year of association membership and say, "I'm out!"

Make this a five year project (minimum)

Senior members of the Society for Marketing Professional Services have told me their biggest frustration is membership turnover just before the SMPS participation really becomes effective. "They quit after two years, not appreciating the longer-range networking value of the association," one executive member told me.

Why does this happen? Your initial enthusiasm (and early welcoming acceptance) has passed, and perhaps you've gathered the low-hanging fruit by marketing to people who are easily visible. Now, if you don't get it right, the slog begins and you seem to be spending your energy with no direct return. This is where people give up.

Obviously, you should listen to your heart and if you simply can't stand the group, get out. However, if the association represents your clients' interests, be careful: The negative vibes you may be feeling towards the association may mirror how your current and potential clients see you!

Moving up the association ladder

After your association contributions are recognized, you will likely be nominated to the local association chapter board of directors. You can then take things further, to leadership at the provincial or state level, or even national or international directorships.

Every time you elevate your association role, you spend more time and energy and receive more marketing value. The reason: Your connections have greater influence and authority, and you can cross-fertilize and test ideas in different markets.

You'll find your calls are returned, and you can make connections and put together deals rapidly because members and colleagues trust you and know you can get the job done. Joint venture projects and supply chain relationships are easy to co-ordinate, and your personal branding and recognition will open otherwise closed doors to you.

Powerful business opportunities

I've enjoyed the results of these association relationships. Huge projects have come together with two or three calls. In one case, a senior association member asked me to lead what turned out to be a highly profitable ongoing project.

I then called other association colleagues to help me put together the proposal and submit the winning bid, which is now earning several tens of thousands of dollars in recurring income.

You win by giving, not receiving

Tim Klabunde, a member of the Society for Marketing Professional Services (SMPS) in the Washington, D.C. area, writes:

Defining Success
As a marketing professional I used to define success as my ability to bring work in the door. Several years ago I came to the conclusion that success did not come down to winning projects, but rather it came down to relationships (through which you can also greatly increase your ability to win work). As I grow, however, I continue to learn and dig deeper into this idea of success.

Success for me... A light came on a couple of years ago when I was reading the networking chapter in Ford Harding's book about rainmaking. In that chapter he reminds us that networking is really just about helping other people. From this simple concept I have developed an approach to networking and life that I believe yields success... I believe that the best way to succeed in life, and business, is to help other people. A life built around helping others will yield not just the joys of relationships, but also the sweet success of achieving your own goals.

Tim is absolutely correct. You build your relationships by giving, sharing, and contributing, not worrying about what you receive. Then, with the relationships in place, opportunities arrive in your inbox. You don't find these opportunities by looking for them, (though, as Ford Harding notes, of course, after a while, you will be able to distinguish the takers from the givers and ease these people out of your network.)

A good test of this principle is when you do a good deed that really helps another association member, and the member responds, "Is there anything I can do for you?"

You'll find the strongest response and powerful relationship building reaction occurs when you say, "No, the only thing I need here is the satisfaction of sharing."

Beware of phoney sincerity

You absolutely must not focus on angling yourself to win business. Nothing is more annoying than the phoney — the person who puts on a superficial air of friendliness and acceptance, then goes in for the kill.

Watch out, also, for the con artist. Just as I recommend association participation to build your relationships, bad people know this as well, and they can ingrain themselves in the association culture. Some of the biggest frauds have been perpetuated through the network effect: Someone buys into a scam and then shares the good news with fellow association members, who trusting the person making the recommendation, sign up as well.

Go beyond your local chapter

Chapter participation is important, but you'll gain the greatest value by looking further afield. You can participate in state or national conventions. Usually these can be tied in with a great vacation which (check with your accountant) you can write off as a business expense.

I've found my writing ability is really helpful here. I volunteered to write some stories for the SMPS national magazine, *The Marketer*. Then *Marketer* Editor Randy Pollock invited me to participate on the national *Marketer* committee. Suddenly, I am able to connect at the highest level, in multiple markets, while doing what I enjoy the most.

Why associations are effective

When you combine your passions and interests with meaningful relationships on a local, regional, and national level, your knowledge expands, and your trust and acceptance increases. Soon, you will have a truly impressive "power network" of people who can help you over rough spots, suggest practical ideas and (best of all) steer business your way.

You will also enjoy your life. Your work, community, and hobbies/interests merge into a holistic picture. You wake up each morning looking forward to the day, and go to bed at night feeling you've accomplished something meaningful.

The basic association rules, revisited

Here, again, are the basic rules for association participation:
- Participate in associations where the majority of membership are among your current/potential clients.
- Don't be intimidated by high dues. If dues are very low, you may find less commitment and long-term value. However, don't throw your money away on sponsorships and advertising.
- Participate right away in activities you enjoy and care about; these can be social as well as business-related. You can take a leadership role relatively early if you contribute where your interests and passions are greatest. The doors are open to your ideas and enthusiasm.
- Be patient. Association participation takes time.
- Share. Focus on giving rather than receiving. Association payoffs are indirect and rarely occur by a measured, strategic involvement. This differs from your other marketing initiatives. But your rewards are usually much larger and longer-lasting.

One warning: Don't lose touch with your own business

Some consultants, including Michael Stone and Bill Caswell, warn of a danger from association participation. You can get so deeply involved in the associations you forget or lose touch with your own business. Your association leadership may be such an enjoyable distraction that you fail to see underlying issues and problems within your own client service, employee relationships, and business finances, and your own business begins to crumble.

You need to mind your own shop, and most importantly, once you reach the level of seniority within the associations that your workload with them is growing, ensure that you delegate responsibilities to other members and the associations' staff.

Keeping things in perspective

Nevertheless, I know successful business owners who have retained their sense of balance and benefited tremendously from their association participation, even in the hardest of times. In Ottawa, for example, Robert Merkley of Merkley Supply served as the leader of two major construction associations simultaneously, during the harsh early 1990s recession. This helped cement his business supplying brick and masonry to contractors within the local community.

Take a few minutes to review these chapters, and think about the associations which reflect the interests of your current and potential clients. Then get involved doing what you like doing the most. In time, you will receive the rewards, and they will be far greater than most conventional marketing approaches.

Chapter 4

The wired (or wireless) world: How to put on-line resources to work for your business

Making money fast (not)

Can you make money fast on the Internet? Well, maybe. Yes, things can happen quickly in the on-line world and you may achieve some impressive marketing results early in your initiatives. However, if you expect immediate payoff from your investment and effort you will likely be disappointed. Internet scams offer "easy money, fast"; real Internet marketing success leads to real relationships, slow.

Internet marketing includes your business website, blog, participation in discussion forums and social e-networking sites, and (in some cases) pay-per-click advertising. The Internet of course also is a great market research resource – you can mine the data available to be much more successful when you are determining priorities, establishing relationships, or checking credentials.

Fast assessment, slow results

The biggest challenge with Internet marketing is when you want things to happen too quickly, your urge for immediate gratification. The second biggest challenge is spending your time and money carelessly without recognizing the Internet's biggest advantage: Your ability to quickly measure and assess your progress. You need to read the signs quickly and adapt your approaches with almost instantaneous feedback.

Yes, you probably noticed the contradictions in the previous paragraph. You need to quickly measure and assess your results, but the results you achieve, at least initially, will be steps on the road to marketing success – not the answers themselves. For example, I could see some people reading and responding to the *Construction Marketing Ideas* blog shortly after starting the project, and knew things were changing when it started skyrocketing in Google's search engine rankings about eight months after beginning the project. However, the first tangible and directly attributed business from the blog and Internet marketing took at least a year to achieve.

Real relationships for real business

Almost inevitably, if you think short term, you will be disappointed. For example, you spend many thousands of dollars (and much time) building the "perfect" website, and you track few visitors and results when you turn it on. On the other hand, you may fall for various scams and ploys to artificially increase your search engine ranking, only to find your business is banished to a permanent sandbox, a lonely spot in the search engine hiearchy that virtually ensures no one will see your website.

The Internet works best when you connect the relationships originally established online with real face-to-face contact and communications. I can trace virtually every significant sale conversion when we went beyond online communication to the phone or, better, an in-person meeting. Then, with your relationships established, you return online, using email and Internet technologies to expedite and facilitate communications, knowing when emails work best or other methods of communication are more effective.

Measure quickly but be patient

Review your daily visitor logs, study your mico-data, and see who is responding to your Internet marketing and who is not. If nothing is happening at all, or the wrong people are responding, change course, quickly. When the time is right, you will sometimes see "instant" sales of incredible value, but you need to combine your analysis with patience. Play quickly, but for long-term results, or you will likely be disappointed or, worse, scammed.

Chapter 5

Internet foundations:
Your domain and website

Editor's note: Much of this chapter's content is elementary. I've included it because you may need a grounding in the basics before you can use more advanced Internet marketing resources.

Selecting your Internet domain name

Your domain – your Internet address – is your least expensive online investment. You can pay as little as $10 a year with online services such as Godaddy. You will pay more if you want personal service and hand-holding but domains should not cost more than $25.00 annually.

This means you can register more than one domain, both to prevent cybersquatting (the borrowing of your internet identity by outsiders) and to try out various ideas for size.

Your domain suffix

Most businesses in North America use .com addresses. Sometimes you can work with .org or .net suffixes and, if your business is outside the U.S., you can use your national suffix (in Canada, this is .ca). I don't think you should use suffixes like .biz and .info, except to prevent copy-cat cybersquatters, because these suffixes imply cheapness.

Your prefix

Long ago, businesses and organizations grabbed the really short prefixes with three or four letters. As well, obvious names are probably taken, especially in major cities. However, you should be able to discover a domain that accurately reflects your business, is easy to remember and isn't too easy to misspell. You can research whether domains are already registered by using search services such as Whois? (www.whois.com).

Your website – the basics

Your website serves several purposes. It is your company's electronic brochure and is likely the first place potential clients will visit when they hear about you. It also can be a resource for current clients, suppliers, and employees, sometimes with a password-protected portal for employees and suppliers to co-ordinate projects.

Your website can be simple or sophisticated. It is worth effort, energy and care. Your website will reflect your business's values and brand: A high-end architectural firm requires a different style than a practical, down-to-earth sub trade. As a rule, you should not sacrifice design for functionality.

Finding a designer

Your designer can be a local student, an offshore service provider (you can obtain surprisingly low bids from services such as Elance (www.elance.com), or a professional design and hosting firm. Many residential contractors have reported great results with Footbridge Media (www.footbridgemedia.com). Footbridge guarantees exclusivity within local market areas for different trades so you don't need to worry about your competition using their services.

Give and take

Give as much value to readers on your website as possible, including useful insights and ideas.

For example, see Mel Lester's The Business Edge (www.bizedge. biz). Lester breaks some rules I advocate here: He uses a .biz domain and his site is far too wordy for my taste, but these limitations are offset by the information he conveys.

Graphic and video images are helpful. Show your quality and scope. Your website should reflect your brand. If you are a wild and wacky organization that likes to have fun with your clients, express these qualities. If you are cautious, safe, and reliable, have a conservative site.

Penny wise: Pound foolish (maybe)

A few years ago, I tried to produce a relatively complicated website with limited resources. I contracted with a designer in India and coder in Pakistan and co-ordinated the project from Canada through overnight Internet messages.

Unfortunately, the final site never worked very well. The design and coding elements failed to mesh properly and I had little recourse to create functionality from the offshore providers once they had received their money.

Next, in another cash-savings initiative, I contracted with a local start-up Internet Service Provider to provide website design and coding in exchange for advertising in our printed publications. The project took more than a year to complete and while we received a functional site, the design was not state-of-the-art.

These failed efforts at cost-savings suggest that you will be better off paying more for a well-recommended designer in your own community.

There is an argument for going cheap, however, Many times, using offshore services, you can receive a great design and functional website, for very little money. (See, for example, The Design and Construction Report site at dcnreport.com, which we had built for $110.00).

If the first effort fails, you just try again. Be wary of spending large sums of money on website design and development. Even with a local designer, you should not need to spend more than a couple of thousand dollars for a sophisticated site or a few hundred dollars for a simple one.

Your site can be a blog

Probably the least expensive way to build a site rapidly is to start a blog – not for the conventional blogging purpose described elsewhere (see page 106), but to serve as your interim home page. Templates provided by Blogger and Wordpress allow you to mix and match components and you (or a high school student in your neighbourhood) can put together a functional blog/site in hours.

Realistic expectations

Once your site is ready, few people will visit it without marketing effort. It takes time, patience and frequent updating to attract search engine recognition. Avoid services promising to elevate your search engine status. They are usually ineffective. You can plan pay-per-click advertising campaigns to attract visitors, but you should only do this if you are confident you can measure the leads you generate and trace the business you earn from the advertising investment.

Attracting website visitors

Promote your new website with email or postal communications to current clients, truck lettering, your business cards and brochures, Once people find your site, encourage them to stay with useful information, video clips, and testimonials. The longer they linger, the more likely they are to do business with you.

Constant change

Frequently, you will need to update your website with new features and capacities. Because websites are relatively inexpensive, you can budget the costs in your planning cycle. A great website is one of your least expensive and most effective marketing investments. Give it priority.

Chapter 6

Online marketing ideas:
The changing environment

Few areas of construction marketing are changing as rapidly as online methodologies. This book section, which reports on resources including websites, blogs, emails, and social networking sites, reflects the rapidly evolving environment.

Construction Marketing Ideas is published with online print-on-demand technologies. I anticipate the chapters here will be updated frequently, and the copy you receive will be different than the words someone else reads six, or even three months from now. I can simply produce the new text and upload the revised layout and chapters to the server. The revised edition is ready within hours. (I'll be happy to send you updates without charge as they are published. Simply email marketingbook@constructionmarketingideas.com to make your request.)

In the following chapters, I'll look more closely at the specific areas of online marketing and how you can apply these resources to your business. Note that advice here can both be extremely timely or extremely dated, depending on where you are in the marketing spectrum and how you apply it.

Here are some ground rules and observations.

Your budget: Money helps but is easy to waste

Online marketing is a great equalizer. You can achieve incredibly effective results for virtually no money, or you can spend a small fortune on outdated approaches and methodologies. For example, the executive officer at one trade association expressed dismay that I had spent money and effort in arranging a website design for a publication where the association would share in the net profits. He had spent $20,000 on a website that had proved to be barely functional and thought I had spent the same.

When I told him that the offshore provider I used had billed me $500.00, his mood changed, and he asked his staff person to work with me on a similar solution. In the end, within two months, the association posted a top-quality new website for less than $1,000.

On the other hand, money can buy you resources to speed up your e-marketing success. If you are careful, and use proper diligence, you can connect with top-notch consultants and designers who, while expensive, give you the leading edge results you desire. As well, some services will co-ordinate your pay-per-click and other online advertising at costs comparable to the Yellow Pages, but with much greater effectiveness. You'll spend a significant amount of money but receive measurable results in return.

You don't need to be a technological guru, but you do need to embrace the technologies

No one expects you to be a web designer, HTML coder, or network administrator. You can hire these services, or in many cases, use off-the-shelf resources. If your budget is low, you can contract for off-shore service providers such as Elance.

However, I believe some hands-on experience is helpful, and you can certainly write your own blog (if you have some writing ability), and join in the social networking site discussions. You need to become involved to truly understand and relate to concepts like social networking and blogging. If you are confused or lack basic knowledge, most likely you are old enough to have children in their teens or at college age. Ask them to show you the ropes.

Frontiers create opportunities

Online marketing resources allow you to break through to success at an incredible speed, especially if you serve a medium-sized or smaller community or work within a highly defined niche. You can quickly implement marketing methodologies to put you in first place within the search engines and your client's perceptions of your business. As well, you can economically develop much smaller and more geographically diverse niches than ever before.

Measuring is easy and rapid

Most online marketing resources are incredibly easy to measure. You can tell how many people are visiting your website, reading your emails, and connecting to your social networking group. You can often know exactly who is expressing some interest, allowing you to build out follow-up campaigns. You can test variations and alternatives instantly.

You can integrate online and off-line marketing

Online marketing sometimes, but rarely, works in isolation from other methods, including phone and face-to-face conversations. However, you can quickly combine the resources. You will find, for example, your ability to network increases exponentially, but you will achieve the greatest results when you relate the online communities to off-line events and activities.

Getting started: Your first step is to take action

You can improve your website, start a blog, and connect within social networking groups within weeks, or in some cases, minutes. Explore the space. You don't need to rush into anything. Sometimes it is best to be quiet and look around you before doing anything, while you experiment and learn before making a public splash. Remember that most websites and blogs initially have virtually no readership or traffic, so if you get it wrong, or wish to try something different, you won't suffer negative consequences.

You also need some patience. While you can speed up the process with money (through paid advertising), most online methodologies take some time to achieve results, just like off-line marketing methods. But you won't go anywhere, ever, if you don't start now. Take some risks.

Chapter 7

Search Engine Optimization: How to (really) achieve to top spot on Google

How important is it for your architectural, engineering or construction business to be in first place with relevant keywords for organic Google searches?

The answer is "very" if you consider two important elements, the percentage of searches that rely on Google, and the amount of attention given to the top position on the search rank compared with others, even on the first page of organic search listings, at least if you believe one widely quoted study from Cornell University researchers Laura A. Granka, Thorsten Joachims and Geri Gay.

The Cornell study using student volunteers discovered that 56.26 per cent of people click on the first organic listing, and the number of clicks declined to 13.45 per cent for second place and 9.82 per cent at third place. Near the bottom, the 10th ranked spot attracts 2.55 per cent and the 7th ranked is in a kind of black hole, at 0.36. Nevertheless, if you are in the top three spots, you have an advantage in two ways: First, 79.63 per will click within the first three places, and they will spend 68.23 per cent of their time there.

Google and other engines

How important is Google in relationship to other search alternatives? According to comScore, in June 2009, Google had close to two thirds of the search market at 65 per cent, followed by Yahoo at 19.6 per cent and Microsoft's new Bing at 8.4 per cent. (Bing is gaining ground, rapidly, in local search, but has yet to truly displace Google or Yahoo.)

If you extrapolate this data, you can see how important it is to have top spot on Google — more than 35 per cent of the total search volume from all engines and sources occurs if you are lucky enough to be first there.

However, I wouldn't ignore the other search engines: Competition is fierce and depending on your community or market segment, other engines may be taking the lead. Keep your mind open.

Getting there

Until recently, many businesses fought to achieve top ranking on the Yellow Pages, creating inventive names like A-A-A1Ardavark Contractors Ltd. These days, they manipulate to achieve similar Internet search engine status. First place means more leads and more business.

However, remember two things: First, the number of leads is less important than their quality, and second, you rarely can find fast and quick solutions here, unless you are willing to pay for your search advertising.

How search engines work

Search engines have similarities to traditional newspaper and free broadcast media. They deliver truly great value to users, at virtually no cost, and attract millions of inquiries each day. In return, they sell advertising, much like the free (to users) Yellow Pages, inexpensive or free newspapers or printed trade publications.

The search engines have the same challenges in managing their free space/services as conventional publishers: Many businesses try to game the system to enhance their own interests. In traditional media, public relations and media specialists try to plant positive news stories and, as I noted previously, businesses rename themselves to receive free top-of-category Yellow Pages listings.

Publishers and search engines fight this gaming. Press releases land in the trash, Yellow Pages publishers set tight geographical restrictions on free listings and Google changes its algorithms to displace sites when it discovers tricks are used to artificially influence results. Sometimes tricks work for a while, but usually, unless your site is truly interesting, relevant and useful, the only way you can get to Page 1 is to pay for sponsored links (more on these later).

The strongest search engine strategy – Relevant and useful content

Google revolutionized the advertising industry by changing information searching rules. The number and quality of back links your website receives is the key to assessing its relevance, interest and utility. The linking concept is elegant in its simplicity: If enough people think your site is worthy, many will link to it, so it is worthy of a high search engine ranking.

The best solution: Original, useful content

If you provide useful, relevant content on your site that is not self-promotional, you will attract links, readers, and higher search engine rankings.

This generosity has an added value: You increase your credibility and introduce your potential clients to your skills and capacities. So, if you are a plumber, include some basic insights into some do-it-yourself (and when not to do-it-yourself) solutions; if you are a renovator, provide helpful design tips; if you are a general contractor, provide explanations about how owners can really build better buildings.

Maturity and updates

The search engines like long-established domains/presence. When you renew your domain, commit for two, three or five years, not one. The additional cost is insignificant. You should also update your site frequently, at least monthly and preferably weekly or even daily. Blogs are helpful (see below.)

Google Local and Bing

Google is trying to increase its relevance and utility at a local level, and in the process has given businesses that are foresighted enough to take advantage of the opportunity, a free ride on the search engine system. Just register key business information with Google Local Business Center. If you are there first, you get extra points, no matter who or what follows you. So go there.

The local search engine market – relevant for most businesses which serve specific geographic areas rather than the entire nation – is evolving rapidly and is currently the biggest frontier in the marketing battle between search engines and other media. Microsoft's Bing algorithms appear to be be reducing Google's dominance for Local Search, but the story may be different in the next few months.

Start a blog and maintain it

I'll cover blogging in greater detail in the next section, but informative blogs (in addition to other uses) have real search engine ranking because the search engines seem to seek them out and blogs attract useful back links.

Write news releases

You'll find more information about news releases elsewhere in this book. You can set them with back links to your website, and submit them to several free or low-cost online news release services. Your search engine rankings will improve.

Giving, not taking, works best in the long run

As you obtain the best networking results by putting others first, the same principle applies winning search engine links. When I started the *Construction Marketing Ideas* blog, I offered free one-way links to blogs related to the topic, without expecting return links. Of course, some thankful people started returning the favour and soon, as the blog's reputation grew, people began calling me (an obvious goal of any marketer!)

Participate in forums

You can share insights within Internet forums in your client market community. Don't barge in with commercial messages and self-promotional stuff, but focus on providing helpful, useful knowledge and be respectful of the forum culture.

You need to be patient here, and give rather than take, but once you are accepted as a full member of the community, no one will mind your signature line and postings including links back to your own site.

Patience pays (unless you wish to pay)

If you want free publicity and organic (natural) high search engine rankings, you will need to be patient. Google, for example, has a sandbox rule for new sites and domains. They don't announce how long it lasts, but you could be banished from visibility for upwards of a year. To see an indication of your sandbox status, key in (on the search engine) your complete domain name. If you find references, but absolutely no sign of your site/domain elsewhere in the search engine references, this means that the search engine knows you are there, but isn't allowing anyone to find you.

The sandbox serves two purposes. One: It prevents gamers from loading up the Internet with manufactured domains and phoney referral sites; and Two: It forces you to pay for your search engine placement through advertising if you aren't willing to wait.

Be patient. Most sites are released from the sandbox within three months to a year. Use this invisible time to improve your site's quality, relevance, and content, rather than worrying about how to find back links or raise your ranking.

Use experts

You can (and probably should, unless you enjoy this type of activity) delegate site development and search engine optimization work to someone else.

I've referenced Footbridge Media as a useful resource. You may find relevant forums. You can connect with other talented people and organizations through your local networks and associations. You can also email me at buckshon@cnrgp.com for some observations and recommendations.

Remember, a high search engine ranking is a means to the end, not the end itself

What good is a great search engine ranking when, after someone calls your number or sends you an email, you fail to respond? Search engine success – or any marketing for that matter – won't help if you or your employees deliver shoddy service. If you conduct your business well, you will receive testimonials and positive back links from truly satisfied clients.

How to go to the top of Google Local in under one month

From Louisville, KY Painting on Contractor Talk

I've lurked on these boards for quite a while now, and have learned a lot about the painting industry, websites, and SEO from you guys.

So as repayment I'll tell you how I went from being ranked somewhere below 200th place to the top spot on Google local in under two weeks.

It's easy and only takes one day.

1) Go to your Google local ad, and click on the edit function. When you get there fill out every bit of it.
2) Provide an address in the city you want to advertise in along with the zip code.
3) Provide four phone numbers one being your fax line.
4) They provide a section where you can list a coupon. Provide the coupon!
5) Fill out the payments accepted field.
6) Fill out the hours of operation
7) In the product and services field? Use it as a keyword bedding area.
8) Get a customer to go provide a review. (I need to do this)
9) They provide an area where you can put up eight images. Do it even if you're using stock images like me. You can take them down and put up your own images when you get them.
10) Last but not least, if you have a video you can load that up too.

I did all these things except the video, and two weeks later a friend that owns one of the largest painting services in the area calls one morning and asks: "Did you know that you're number one on Google Local now? How did you do that?"

I almost fell over.

Chapter 8

Blogging: How, why and when

If you enjoy writing and wish to share your heartfelt opinions and passions, blogs provide a unique and truly effective marketing resource for your business. Blogging is not for everyone. In fact, most people in the construction industry should not blog. You need to be able to write fast, well, and creatively.

Unlike most other skills, you cannot delegate the task unless you wish to grant your employees freedom to blog in their own names. This requires you to allow them to enter public spaces on the company's behalf, without your looking over their shoulders and editing every word. Most employees will be afraid to go out on a meaningful limb unless you set the example.

If you enjoy blogging and do it right, you may find your blog is one of your most effective marketing resources. It gives your business a public personality you wouldn't achieve otherwise, and you will find productive sales leads, along with enhanced employee and client loyalty and better brand recognition.

Easy to start

Blogs are easy to start. Many bloggers rely on Google's Blogger service (www.blogger.com) or the readily available WordPress (www.wordpress.org) templates, which you can host on your own server. With Blogger, you simply enter the system, sign in, and then build your blog from templates provided. You can set up a basic blog in minutes – in fact, you can use this as an interim web page if you are just getting started.

Harder to maintain

The challenge with blogging is to continue to provide fresh, relevant content. Really good blogs are updated daily (sometimes more than once a day); I don't know many blogs that work well without at least a weekly update. Most blogs start optimistically, then fizzle out. If you are like most start-up bloggers, you are are either distracted by other interests or challenges or (perhaps more significantly), your early blog entries don't seem to have much impact. You may feel you are writing for an audience of one (yourself!)

Habit forming success and relationships

If you are fortunate to enjoy blogging (I do), really good things eventually happen, though you will hit some bumps on the road. About eight months after I started the blog, I received a disturbing email from Google/Blogger saying my blog would be suspended pending manual review. It seems that Google, knowing about spam blogs (or splogs) to build search engine back links, has systems in place to require human intervention/observation when the number of links back to any blog reach a certain level. After someone at Google inspected my blog personally, my blog search engine rankings skyrocketed. I found, to my pleasant surprise, that my blog now has number one spot on keywords such as "Construction Marketing"

This high search engine ranking, of course, is helpful, but the really good stuff occurs when I connect either by phone or at conventions or meetings with other relevant bloggers, especially within the Society for Marketing Professional Services (SMPS). With the blog, my business network has increased dramatically, creating new opportunities and valuable business-referencing relationships. You can achieve the same level of success, if you are patient and committed to effective blogging.

Blogging and employees

Allowing and encouraging your employees to blog helps to create a more open business culture, especially when your employee blogs reflect your business values and relevance to current, former, and potential clients. Of course, you should not force your employees to blog. Nor should you edit the blog postings or direct your employees about what to say or do, unless of course they are violating laws, causing offence, or publishing your trade secrets!

If you own the business or are responsible for hiring, your blog will be a useful introduction to qualified people who may want to know more about you before joining your organization.

Blog comments

Comments, of course, are where readers interact with you and great blogs attract many comments. Don't expect too many comments at the start – some studies show that on average 100 people will view a blog for one person to comment. Some spammers and commercial services will try to load comments on your site; you need to review and edit these out (most blog software makes this easy). You can, of course, submit your own comments as a response to a comment or to clarify a detail on your original blog posting.

Copyright and images

You should always respect copyright. Generally, you aren't risking copyright violations by providing direct links back to the sites to which you are referring (and most site owners will be happy to receive your search-engine-boosting one-way link). However, you should not use images or significant portions of text without permission. Stock image services such as Istockphoto (www.istockphoto.com) are helpful: You can purchase a low resolution image (suitable for your blog) for $1.00. If you lift something from someone else's site, you can also simply send an email and request permission. Usually the person will agree, especially since your link to their site has value to them.

Editing and review

You should of course think before you post, but you don't need the meticulous care as when you are writing a printed book or preparing a sophisticated corporate video. The reason: Blogs have built in editing functions. You can generally revise or delete your postings when you think it necessary.

Beware, of course, of the archiving functions on the Internet: Your work doesn't necessarily disappear even after you hit "delete." You should therefore be extra cautious before posting anything that is contentious, controversial, or might damage the reputation of someone else (generally a dumb marketing practice, anyway). It never hurts to sleep on it if you are in doubt, or show your draft posting to a friend or colleague for feedback.

However, don't get too fussy here. Blogs work best when they have some spontaneity and genuineness. This means they aren't always perfect, but if your message doesn't have the edge of authenticity, if it isn't really the way you speak and act in normal life, people will turn off quickly, and you might as well spend your time doing something else.

The Wordpress advantage

For the first three years of my blog, several people asked me why I didn't maintain the blog on my own server using templates from the voluntary WordPress.org community (not to be confused with Wordpress.com). I demurred, noticing the rising level of recognition of the existing Blogger account, but finally braved the switch at Christmas time, 2009-2010.

With more recent experience, I can recommend, if you are comfortable with the initial start-up challenges, that you start your blog on your own hosted or controlled server with WordPress.org rather than Blogger or other externally hosted services (including Wordpress.com.)

The reason is you will have much greater depth and control. With a diversity of freely available "plugins" and themes, you will be able to control and manage your site's appearance and content with relative ease.

The best way to go, if you are uncertain, is to look at some great blogs you like and then communicate with the blogger(s) for some guidance. Once you've set up your site, you can often search for solutions using simple Google inquiries.

If you are totally unsure and afraid of anything to do with technology, don't despair. The commercial sites such as Blogger will still allow you to develop an effective and useful blog. However, a little time at start-up will save you some headaches later. I'm faced with maintaining an otherwise-unused Blogger site to preserve my search engine status until the new blog catches up sufficiently in the rankings and recognition.

Your own blog

When you start your blog, let me know. Share the news and email buckshon@cnrgp.com. If it is relevant to construction industry marketing, I'll include it in the *Construction Marketing Ideas* blog links list. No need to reciprocate, but your blog's search engine ranking will certainly improve.

Chapter 9

Advertising: When it works, when it won't

Should you advertise? Since my business earns 95 per cent of its revenue from advertising, you might expect a totally biased answer: "Yes." However, I realize that advertising, while a useful resource in many situations, is not the magic answer for most construction industry marketers. You need to know when and how to advertise before spending your hard-earned money. You need to be wary about any sales representative who suggests advertising in their publication, directory, or electronic media will provide a quick fix to your marketing problems.

Consider the results of the *Construction Marketing Ideas* poll, which shows that 74 per cent of construction companies discover most of their new business through repeat and referral relationships.

Only 10 per cent say advertising is their major source of new business. These results are significant, because advertising can be truly costly. You can spend hundreds, even thousands of dollars on a single print ad, for example, and receive not a single call in return. The money just disappears.

Measuring your results and controlling your costs

Still, advertising has real advantages if you can manage and measure your results and control your costs. With an effective advertising campaign you will enhance your brand and attract new clients and, if you know what you are doing, you can dial up or down your advertising volume to ensure a steady flow of qualified leads, a real advantage in a recession. With online and pay-per-click or inquiry advertising, you also can avoid one of the biggest problems of conventional advertising, the need to commit large sums of money upfront for uncertain results.

Other advertising methods, including print media trade publications (like ours), trade/home shows, direct mail and electronic newsletters, and even the Yellow Pages, have their advantages, in certain circumstances. I'll explain these in the pages ahead.

Why not rely on referral and repeat business?

Consultant Michael Stone believes too many contractors rely too much on referral and repeat relationships, and advertise too little. He has a point, in that if your advertising campaign is well designed and correlates solidly to a proper sales lead and calculation process, you can measure your results effectively and then control your flow of business by attracting new leads and reminding former clients of your presence.

Stone's point is that relying passively on repeat and referral business is a recipe for business disaster, especially in hard times. You can of course design your advertising to enhance and encourage repeat and referral orders – and this will probably be the most effective advertising you can do. You should, as your first priority, engage your previous clients in your advertising and systematically encourage them to refer new business to you. (See Chapter 2-1 for more observations here).

How much should you spend on advertising?

Stone advocates that you advertise in at least six different ways and observes that contractors, on average, need to spend at least 5 per cent of their overall sales on advertising. However, his definition of "advertising" is broader than mine. The 5 per cent number is valid for overall organized marketing initiatives rather than just conventional paid advertising. (He counts your website and business cards, along with organized referral and repeat business development to come up with the 5 per cent recommendation. I would add organized media relations and association membership fees to this total.)

This suggests if you are a contractor with about $1 million in business volume you should budget about $50,000 for systematized marketing and advertising. If your business is expanding into new areas, you will need to spend a higher percentage than if you are maintaining your business/brand and, if you are just starting up, you will need your expense to be much more in sweat than cash if you are to remain in business for any length of time.

You may find you can achieve great results with relatively modest advertising investments. Consider that retailing giant Wal-Mart and its strongest competitors allocate 2 per cent or less of their revenues on advertising. Regardless, it is wise to have a budget and to plan your expense.

Consider your current clients first

Besides engaging your current clients in referral and repeat marketing initiatives, which will provide you the highest return on your marketing investment, consider asking them to tell you which media they read, watch, and respect. Similarly, check with non-competitive peers in other markets similar to yours demographically, either through online forums or (often more effectively) through your trade association network. You may find you can combine this research with a family vacation and write off many of your travel costs. Certain types of media work well in some markets, rather than others. For example, a glossy high end magazine may produce great results for home renovations in Atlanta, but a similar publication might be ineffective in Boston. You need to learn from your clients and colleagues what is most likely to work – and what won't – before communicating with advertising sales representatives.

Where advertising really works

Advertising can be effective in these circumstances:

You provide a specific service that fills an occasional need – If you are a roofer, sell windows and doors, pave driveways or install siding, clients need your services occasionally and in emergency situations. Advertising can help you capture this business when they are ready.

You wish to maintain and enhance relationships with your existing clients – My business sells most of its advertising this way. Construction-related businesses work with us on special editorial publicity feature profiles (see the section about publicity and media relationships) and, with their consent, we sell advertising to the featured companies' suppliers. Here, the advertising message supports your existing client relationships, while expanding your credibility through a positive association: "We're good enough to supply this credible business, so we must be good enough for you."

You are protecting and preserving your brand – This is the type of advertising that may, on the surface, seem to be the most expensive and least effective. I believe media outlets thrive on this soft advertising since often large and expensive ongoing brand-focused advertising campaigns generate little in measurable, additional sales. Nevertheless, done right, and in conjunction with other strategies that ensure your clients are served and treated well, this form of advertising can increase competitive market entry barriers and help you preserve and enhance your marketing power. You can also score strategic successes against your competition if you use brand-focused marketing with natural word-of-mouth and high product/service quality. (Consider the successful Apple advertising campaign poking fun at the nerdy, bloated, Microsoft Windows/Vista operating systems.)

When advertising doesn't work

Advertising is rarely effective when:

You fail to test, measure, or understand why you are advertising – I've seen much money wasted on advertising, especially in low circulation, poorly produced publications that no one reads. Recently, I analysed some so-called police journals sold by telemarketers. The police associations may receive small referral fees, but the magazines have little content or relevance to law enforcement officers. I discovered these ineffective publications earn most of their advertising revenue from local construction businesses. Maybe the advertising contractors and sub trades hope for more police protection, but I can't see how lining the pockets of telemarketers really helps your business security. This advertising certainly wastes your marketing budgets.

You offer a professional or business-to-business service (unless framed in an editorial context) – Although some large engineers, architects, and lawyers advertise to support their brand, this is expensive and your money could better be directed to improving your client experience, recruiting top notch professionals, and increasing your trade association/group marketing activities.

The exception to this rule is when you discover a valid linkage between advertising and editorial publicity, the "advertorial." In the right media (and this should only be in high quality publications distributed to the people you really want to reach), these advertorials can provide credibility for your professional practice while allowing you content and scheduling control unavailable in regular editorial coverage. However, you should be satisfied that the media reaches and is respected by your current and potential clients before rushing into any campaigns.

You are sold advertising, rather than purchase it – Most of the time, you should initiate rather than accept unsolicited inquiries from advertising media. You need to plan and strategically consider how and when to advertise, not respond to media representative promises. You also need to test their credibility. Do they have real evidence of their media's effectiveness, value, and reliability? A good way to separate the phoney sales claims from real results is to ask if the publication or media outlet will stand behind their claims and guarantee results. Most will come up with excuses to decline such a commitment. A few will take the risk, knowing they are effective, or at least they will provide you with enough of an overall value commitment that you can be confident that you will receive your money's worth for your advertising investment. (This is our philosophy, and is part of the reason behind this book. Our advertisers will, on request, receive enough independent free marketing consulting services to more than offset their advertising investment with us, regardless of immediate results.)

Leave 10 per cent for extras

While you should plan your advertising and be generally wary of inbound media sales inquiries, when you set your annual advertising budget, keep some money aside for special circumstances: The off-the-wall idea might just work, or you may want to publish some advertising in support of your best clients. A good rule of thumb is to reserve about 10 per cent for spontaneous and non-budgeted advertising options. This gives you room to try out new media during the year, without tearing apart existing campaigns.

Maintaining your discipline in hard times

When economic conditions deteriorate, you may be tempted to pour money into advertising to find new business or to cut your advertising budget drastically to preserve cash flow. Both solutions are generally unwise. You should of course review your expenses. You may have habitually continued advertising in ineffective media and can wisely reallocate your resources. As well, you will need to begin planning advertising if you are to survive hard times: Just think things through carefully. If the advertising costs a significant amount of money, satisfy yourself that you will really reach your clients and that you know similar advertising is effective for non-competitive businesses in markets similar to yours.

In the next chapter, I'll give you some suggestions for getting better results with less money, from your advertising, and how to decide which media to use, and when.

Chapter 10

Some effective advertising suggestions

Do you want your advertising to enhance your brand, attract sales leads, or both? Most architectural, engineering and construction businesses want to generate real business. It is hard to measure the value of institutional or brand-maintenance advertising. Instead of advertising to maintain your brand, why not improve the client experience?

Nevertheless, once you discover an effective advertising formula, you will find it helpful in stabilizing and growing your business, allowing you to generate profitable leads even in challenging economic environments.

Advertising and your suppliers: A note about co-op advertising

It is always wise to ask your suppliers for assistance with your advertising and marketing. Many have organized co-op programs, and others will provide resources on a case-by-case basis. Some suppliers relate their co-op support to the amount of business you do with them. In other cases, the quality of your relationship may be the most important dimension. This money is there if you ask, but it often sits on the table, untouched, if you don't. When your suppliers help pay your advertising costs, you have a real competitive edge.

Long versus short term

You need to create 9 to 13 impressions with potential new clients before you receive business. These impressions can be from advertisements, email letters, truck signs, direct mailing pieces, and phone conversations. One-time ads rarely work, unless you are selling something highly specific to someone already looking for your service (the traditional classified ad).

This is why media representatives encourage you to lock in to longer campaigns. They know that if your advertising is too infrequent, it won't generate the leads you are seeking and you will think the advertising has failed.

These principles create a paradox: You need to commit significant resources without being sure you will achieve results. In fact, many campaigns fail, even after multiple impressions. You are back to the drawing board until you find something that works.

Reducing the risks: Planning and testing alternatives

Obviously this is a costly trial-and-error approach, but it isn't too bad, if you think long-term. You simply need to find one formula that works and build on it. The challenge is this can be hard to do when things aren't going well, which is why it is wisest to begin planning your advertising when you think you have enough business and then the initial failures won't strain your resources. (If you are starting in tough conditions, I recommend you look at what works for your peers in other markets and copy the models rather than reinvent the wheel.)

Once your advertising is successful, producing profitable leads and results, you can test variations and extensions. For example, if you discover an effective newspaper ad, you can then try other publications or revise the ad's wording to see if you achieve improvements.

This process is practical, sustainable, and repeatable. As time passes, you build a base of effective ads and you can predict your results. Then, if business conditions change, you can increase the advertising to fill your order pipeline. You should never cut your advertising completely even when you have enough work because, if you do, you lose the cumulative effect of your ongoing marketing. Of course, you can scale back your advertising if you are really busy.

How to work with advertising sales representatives

Great advertising sales representatives can guide you. They think long term and may be able to suggest other marketing resources.

How do you find advertising representatives you can trust? You can check with your peers, clients, and suppliers.

Don't rush anything

You should insist that advertising representatives who call you unsolicited, provide you with additional information by email or courier/mail before discussing things further. This usually weeds out dialling-for-dollars telemarketers.

(Note if the advertising representative says he is calling on behalf of one of your clients or a charity or organization you respect, you should verify the claim. Often you will do more good by making a direct contribution than sponsoring a charity-focused publication where most of your money supports the publication, not the charity.)

Commitments and contracts — the rules of the game

Should you lock in long-term advertising agreements? Yes, under certain circumstances but don't do this until you know where you are heading. The Yellow Pages has traditionally been one of the biggest challenges. You need to sign up, pay for a year, and can't change your ad. (I discuss these directories later).

Most media outlets offer soft contracts. That is, you sign up to purchase a certain amount of air time, or number of insertions (or agate lines, referring to the size of the ad – 14 agates equals one inch) and you receive discounts for frequency, repetition and volume.

If conditions change and you wish to cancel or reduce your advertising, you simply pay the difference in the advertising rates for the time you actually advertised. For example, if you contract to purchase an advertisement at $350 per insertion over 12 issues, and the one-time rate is $500.00, if you cancel after your two insertions, most media outlets will allow you out of the deal if you pay the additional $150 x 2 or $300. The converse applies, as well. If you purchase enough advertising, you may be able to obtain a credit for your previous orders. It never hurts to ask.

Advertising media pricing – hard and soft

Media outlets have different rules about pricing. Some won't allow any deviations from their rate schedules; others will bend the rules if you ask nicely (or sometimes, firmly). Thus, it always makes sense to ask if the media outlet can provide a discount, or perhaps some extra time or space, or advertorial support. Often your media representative will be able to suggest alternatives that will save you money or add value. You may receive perks ranging from sports tickets to gift bouquets. Obviously you should not accept these benefits if you would violate your employers' rules, but if you own your business or have authority from your management, you can decide whether the gifts and extras compromise your integrity and business judgement.

Contra-trade and barter advertising

Sometimes, media will be happy to exchange advertising for your goods or services or, if you are supporting a community or non-profit organization, grant you free advertising. These trades can make sense, if you don't incur other unexpected fees as a result. (Booth rental, for example, is only a small part of the cost of attending trade shows. You also need to budget your time, set-up, and other resources.) Linking your business to charity and community service can help your brand, and if the advertising is free, you achieve success without any financial investment.

Organized barter exchanges may be helpful, but you need to be satisfied that the value you receive really matches what you are spending in time and effort. As a rule, unless you truly require the service offered in exchange, I would stick with cash.

The Yellow Pages and directories

Yellow Pages and directory advertising present special challenges. You can't change your ad, and you need to prepay or commit to a sizeable monthly payment, without being sure of your results. You can throw good money into a black hole if you aren't sure of where you are heading.

Obviously, if your business is large enough, you won't be harmed by spending $200 or $300 annually on a directory listing, but what about $1,000 a month or more for a Yellow Pages ad? These days, I see no reason for most businesses to spend this kind of money, especially since many people make their quick-search decisions for immediate needs on the Internet.

Of course, if your current directory or Yellow Pages advertising is effective, continue. Yellow Pages advertising may also be useful in certain locations with older demographics and for trades and services which are required urgently when the power fails.

Some printed directory publishers provide a pay-per-lead or call service, similar to Google's pay-per-click. This can be good value, but when the sales representative suggests you pay a set-up fee, decline. Your cash risk declines, and you will only receive an invoice if the directory provides useful leads. (Note these directories, such as Go Local in Canada, still have a significant disadvantage: If you are paying per call/lead and the calls are not converting to meaningful orders, you are obligated for the cost, while you can simply pull or change your online advertising within days if your advertising is generating inquiries which do not convert to sales.)

Content and format – what to say

In print media, you'll notice three types of advertising: Classified, conventional display, and direct response. Classified and directory-type ads are brief, to-the-point, with abbreviations and sometimes a call to action. They are also relatively inexpensive.

Conventional display advertising usually follows a standard formula. Your headlines should be 9 to 13 words, a graphic image should occupies ⅔ to ¾ of the space, descriptive or message text should usually be in a smaller type at the bottom of the ad, with a (small) business logo and call to action at the end. This formula is used by most agencies for large national advertisers. Read the ads in national magazines and you will see how this is true.

Should you dare to be different? Maybe, but you will probably come out as an amateur. The traditional approach has been tried, tested and proven successful over several decades.

Direct response rules

Direct response advertising follows its own rules. These ads are wordy with virtually no graphics except small supporting illustrations. Writers design the copy to be compelling and they seek to draw you into the story. The longer you read the advertisement, the more likely you are to purchase. Usually, you will find a powerful P.S. message.

Direct response ads are designed with one intent in mind: To get your phone to ring or email to ping. You measure your success by the number of inquiries and their success in converting to orders. Not surprisingly, you may find the direct response advertising model is the wisest route, especially if you are starting your advertising campaign in a challenging economy. However, if you are marketing to high-end demographics be careful as you may degrade your brand.

Your advertising budget

You need to think about how you will spend your advertising dollars and incorporate this expense in your annual plan. A good rule of thumb, as noted before, is to allocate at least 5 per cent of your projected overall sales to marketing and advertising. With your budget, you can decide where and when to advertise, avoiding rash decisions based on emotion or smooth-talking sales representatives.

To determine your cost and net profit per lead, you will certainly want to measure how many calls you receive and the sales conversion rate. This data will be helpful in benchmarking media performance and, most importantly, if you are well organized, allow you to adjust your advertising volume to ensure a steady flow of paying clients.

Chapter 11

The Internet: The new frontier (and opportunity) for advertising

The Internet has revolutionized advertising. Online pay-per-click or per-result advertising is far more effective and much less risky than most conventional advertising, especially television and printed media like the Yellow Pages.

With Google and its competitors, you don't need to pour your advertising dollars into a black hole. Instead, you measure your results instantaneously and only continue if the ads generate worthwhile responses.

Paying for results, not effort

With conventional media, you generally need weeks or even months to measure your advertising's success. Sure, you can place a newspaper classified ad to appear in a day or two, and your local radio station will be happy (for a fee) to rush a promotion on air. But you still have to hope for response. Whether or not anyone calls, the publisher will send you an invoice.

With online media, you select whether to pay per impression or per click, and how much you wish to pay. Google, Bing (Microsoft), Yahoo, and smaller services will then determine how high to place your ad on their search engine pages. Your position is highest if you are willing to pay the most and the largest number of people click on your message.

You will pay more or less depending how many other advertisers are competing, depending on topic, location, and keywords. If you aren't happy with the results, you simply discontinue the ads.

Content networks

You can elect to advertise on co-operating websites in advertising networks along with the search engine sites. For example, your roofing company advertisement may appear near website articles on "how to select a roofer," restricted to Internet users in your community. Google operates the largest content network, but has competitors.

Managing the process

While I encourage you to try Internet search and website advertising to get a feel for the process, you soon will likely contract with specialist agencies who understand the nuances and details. You can easily blow your budget on expensive keywords or inappropriately targeted advertising. If you are currently using media like the Yellow Pages, you may find advertising management agencies can help you switch to web-based media, at a monthly cost similar to or less than you have been paying (and without fixed annual obligations.)

However, before you call the agency, take a few minutes to open a Google AdWords account and explore the concept. You can set small spending limits and work after hours. With some familiarity, you will be much more comfortable communicating with advertising service representatives, and you will also be better able to see through sales representatives' exaggerated claims.

Detailed measurement and analytics

You will quickly notice how much detailed information you can gather about your advertising campaign. You'll know how many people are viewing your web pages, clicking on your ads and, if you configure things correctly, who is purchasing your services.

As I've observed previously, only 10 per cent of construction companies report that advertising is their primary business source. You need every stage of the lead conversion process to be flawless. If your website is not appealing, click-throughs from online ads won't convert into emails or inquiries. If you fail to respond promptly and courteously, you won't convert the inquires into appointments. You must deliver what you promise (and more) to create the word-of-mouth for repeat and referral business.

Specialized forums, websites, and groups

You can also target your message on specialized Internet forums, websites and groups. Some will accept Google content network advertisements, while others will work with you directly or use other advertising management services.

Consider, for example, the story of a major building products manufacturer. He showed me a full page advertisement in an architectural publication that had resulted in no business despite an investment of several thousand dollars. He said some trade shows are effective, at a cost of $75.00 per lead. He then tried AEC Daily (aecdaily.com) and observed leads flowing in shortly after his online advertising started.

His sales team reported the Internet leads converted to orders just as well as the trade show. The price per lead: $7.50, an order of magnitude lower.

Picking your niche

Because the advertising space for your keyword or banner ad online marketing message is highly constrained, you need to combine the right words or visual images with a succinct and effective message. You have many combinations and creative possibilities. You need to think small and big at the same time.

Fortunately, you can control the variables with resources such as the free Google Keyword Tool. Select the keywords of your choice or your site URL, and you will quickly learn about your competition.

I discovered, for example, that on average about 9,000 people search Google monthly for "Construction Marketing." When I asked the tracker to analyse my site for words which might be relevant to my blog, it pointed out "home office" or "business," among others. However, if I chose these words, I would need to budget upwards of $4,000 a day to reach everyone and most inquiries would not be relevant for my specialized market.

Conversely, many keyword options are truly inexpensive. Some may be highly relevant for your business, but it can be a challenge to figure out which ones are best. This is where specialist Internet advertising agencies can be especially helpful. They may suggest words that exactly reach your demographic but are much less expensive than the immediately obvious (and popular) combinations.

To access the Google Keyword tool, visit:
https://adwords.google.com/select/KeywordToolExternal

How long do you need to get results?

Set a modest budget, say $1,000 to $5,000, try the keywords you think will work best and see what happens. If you notice good conversion rates, then you are off to a great start. Experiment with variations. Pay more or less per keyword and try different geographical or format options. You'll know within a few weeks what works best, and this becomes your "control." Then experiment with variations. Overall, you may need a month or more of trial and error before you have confidence in your results.

Search engine optimization, advertising, or both

In the previous chapter, I reviewed some techniques to boost your organic or free listings in Google and other search engines. Should you emphasise your free search rankings or focus on paid advertising? The answer, I believe, is you should do both.

Overall, as news section stories and broadcast programs attract much better results than advertising, free search engine listings (if you reach first or second place) are far more cost effective than expensive paid keyword or content network advertising.

If you achieve high search engine rankings through relevant content and readership interest, you are unlikely to be dislodged as long as you continue improving and updating your site. This work takes much time and effort, and you may need to wait months (or even years) until you achieve success. If a competitor is already there, he is not likely to give up the space without a fight.

Therefore, if you want fast results, use keyword advertising while you improve your site with fresh content. Eventually, you may reach the search engine pinnacle. Then you can redirect your advertising budget to other media as you celebrate your Internet marketing success.

Chapter 12

Canvassing, broadcast faxing and telemarketing: The marketing bad guys

$20,000 for three hours work

Last year, Rob Norton walked down our street, knocking on doors. Since we detest and avoid door-to-door canvassers at our household, we ignored him when he stopped by our house. However, Norton had his one page hand-written flier ready, and he left it at the door.

Vivian, on seeing the amateur writing, crumpled the thing up to throw it out, but I decided to investigate further and phoned him. "I get three weeks work with three hours work" door-knocking and leaving the hand-written photocopied note at houses where he sees signs of water damage in front of the house, he said.

"Probably we drop about 100 fliers — we get 10 to 15 call-backs, and for 10 houses, each house provides between $1,000 and $2,000 worth of work" — that translates to between $10,000 and $20,000 in sales for as little as three hours' effort.

Norton said the handwritten format works best. Many people think each note is personally written, he says. He adds that most of his business comes when he actually speaks to someone at the doorstop, and other business comes from referrals as neighbours see the work being done. However, 20 to 30 per cent of his business is from call-backs from the handwritten photocopied note.

Canvassing: Unprofessional success

I showed the note to a couple of people, and they laughed, amazed at how unprofessional it looks. However, Rob Norton, in the telephone interview, said he is employing a crew of between three and five workers and doing thousands of dollars of business. Norton does not have a website or a published email address. Most of the business for his company, which has been established over the last two years, comes from the door knocking and handwritten note, he said. (I tried to verify the observations in this initial interview with follow-up calls; he declined to make himself available, so possibly he was overstating his success.)

Door-knocking in Columbus: A first-hand investigation

These results intrigued me enough that I decided to investigate the canvassing option further, by contacting canvassing consultant Joseph Needham in Grand Rapids, Michigan. He sells through his website at www.procanvasser.com a manual/disk for about $350 and, if you wish to take things further, he will provide full-scale on-location consulting services. He suggested I visit with him while on a canvassing assignment in Columbus, Ohio, and I spent a day following him and a trainee canvasser around on canvassing program for local contractor Feazel Roofing.

Storms, insurance and canvassing

Feazel Roofing president Mike Feazel says he receives about a third of his business from radio advertising (he has a budget of several hundred thousand dollars a year) and another third from repeat and referral inquiries, with the remainder from a diversity of alternative media. He wants to use canvassing to supplement other services, and when I travelled on site with Joseph Needham, I could see how canvassing can be highly effective if your service meets a need that you can perceive from the street.

Feazel Roofing knows, for example, that certain types of roof damage after hail and wind storms are common for some but not all roof types, and that these may not be obviously visible to homeowners. The contractor also knows these repairs are covered by insurance and that, under local rules, the insurance premiums cannot be increased if you file a claim after a natural disaster. So, here, canvassing makes a lot of sense: Canvassers can explain they can solve homeowners' problems without any cost to them.

The soft sale

Needham says most canvassers are men. He avoids working with anyone who isn't presentable and of good character. Good canvassers are always respectful of the homeowners they visit; they accept "no" for an answer, and won't knock on doors or enter neighbourhoods with "no soliciting" signs. Needham emphasizes that in the U.S., canvassing cannot be unreasonably restricted by local ordinances but that some neighbourhoods are more receptive to canvassers than others.

Telemarketing and broadcast faxing

While canvassing is protected by the U.S. Constitution, telemarketing and broadcast faxing have serious regulatory limitations. Generally, you can use the phone for business-to-business marketing, but you should be very careful about do-not-call-list regulations for consumer phone marketing. In the U.S., unsolicited advertising faxes are subject to severe and onerous Federal Communications Commission regulations. There are exceptions, but if you send out broadcast faxes to anyone with whom you don't have an existing relationship to advertise or promote your business, you could be fined $500 per fax! Obviously, this marketing method should not be used unless you are truly courageous and are sure you are complying with the rules. (The faxing rules are less onerous in Canada, provided you don't fax anyone who asks to be removed from your fax list. Canadians, like U.S. businesses, however, must be wary of do-not-call-list regulations.)

Of course, there is a big difference between telemarketing in a rote, scripted manner, and using the phone (or for that matter the fax or email) to draw out individual business interest based on qualified leads and personal relationships. You may find some value in setting aside a day or two per week for some strategic calling especially to qualify leads and learn about upcoming projects.

Measuring costs and risks against benefits

Most people find canvassing, cold calling and telemarketing stressful and unpleasant. I've noted before that you generally should do things you enjoy and do well, in designing your marketing strategies. Do you need the stress of rejection? Do you want to go through the ordeal of hiring, training, and replacing disgruntled or incompetent employees when you ask others to do these unpleasant tasks. (Worse, if you contract the services out, do you know that the callers or door-knockers will behave with integrity and won't damage your brand and business reputation?)

I believe you should rarely want or need to canvass, cold call or telemarket, though you may find these resources useful in situations where you have a project under-way and wish to engage neighbours in the process (radius marketing) or you have a visibly necessary service and need quick and immediately measurable marketing results (for example, if you are in a business crisis). In these situations, the psychic cost and stress of canvassing and cold calling are offset by the immediate revenue you achieve. However, don't knock on my door!

Chapter 13

The printed media: Traditional resources still work, sometimes

For many years, printed media, including newspapers, Yellow Pages directories, brochures, fliers and printed newsletters represented some of the most cost-effective resources available for construction industry marketers. Print still has its place, but you need to be thoughtful and careful about what you do.

The Yellow Pages

Most young people (and many older people) now rarely review these bulky books, but in some markets, they continue to be effective. Because of the contract requirements for Yellow Pages advertising (you need to sign up and pay for a year's advertising that you cannot change or cancel), I would avoid the Yellow Pages unless you have been using them successfully in the past, when there were no effective online alternatives. If a Yellow Pages ad sales rep calls, say you will be happy to advertise only if you can be guaranteed results.

In some markets, you can achieve this guarantee, with a system of pay-per-response phone listings. In Canada, newspapers publish a pay-per-response directory under the "GoLocal" brand. The publisher sets out a cost per lead depending on your ad size and industry category, and assigns a special phone number to allow electronic tracking of the number of in-bound calls. You only pay for calls, not the listing. (Sales reps will attempt to charge you a design and set up fee; try to negotiate a slightly higher pay-per call fee in place of the design fee.)

Newspapers and Magazines

In most markets, conventional daily newspapers are suffering as advertisers and readers disappear to online media. Some specialized magazines remain effective because of their long shelf life and highly focused demographics. If the magazine relates directly to your market, you may find it effective.

One challenge with print media advertising (outside of daily publications) is the long lead time between placing your advertising and seeing results. You also need multiple impressions to achieve results.

The best strategy with print media advertising is to speak with your current clients and see which media they read, and consider important in their lives. This can vary by market – in some areas, glossy magazines really work well; in others, they don't.

Business-to-business and trade publications

If you are seeking to sell to other businesses, (for example you are a commercial contractor) should you advertise in these media? The key to effective advertising in the trade press is to co-ordinate it with other marketing activities and initiatives of the trade journal publisher. For example, you may be able to negotiate editorial placements or publicity, a position on their website, some e-mail marketing support, guidance and advice on trade shows, and other services. A well-connected trade magazine/newspaper publisher will know where the opportunities are within the relevant industry and can direct you within your market. In other words, the value of advertising in the trade press is much more than the physical insertion order and any results you may achieve from your advertising. If you feel you are getting rote treatment from a sales rep, you should seek someone more senior in the publishing organization for advice.

Your business cards

Yes, this is a basic marketing tool, and you should have some. You can make your cards stand out. Marketing guru Jeffrey Gitomer for example, hands out coins instead of cards. The business card can convey an effective first impression and make it easy for people to contact you. Some authorities say that do-it-yourself quick-printed cards don't convey a very professional image, but they are probably quite adequate if you are a small contractor or sub trade. You won't drain your budget by spending a little more on higher quality cards. Of course, include your contact phones, emails, and website information on the cards.

Should you hand out or mass distribute your cards to everyone, or should you simply give them when requested or when you are actually engaged in business? The answer depends in part on the nature of your business. Most of the time, if you hand out business cards widely, you will achieve little direct response. Maybe you should buy some Google keywords instead.

Brochures and fliers

Some marketers spend hours and weeks trying to get their brochure just right. And, yes, there are right ways to do these things and not-so-right ways. But how good do they really need to be? In the last chapter, I describe how a local contractor knocking on doors uses a handwritten and photocopied note to get thousands of dollars in business. Therefore you should spend some, but not too much time, on this topic.

You can ask designers to build your brochures for you – probably a rational thing if you are more into construction than marketing. Consider Footbridge Media, or if you want to do things yourself, StockLayouts (you can find a link from my blog). The stocklayouts.com service will provide you with templates which you can easily adapt to your local requirements.

Door-hangers and fliers may work in certain circumstances. Again, check with non-competing businesses in other markets, or with your current and previous clients to learn what they find effective.

Direct mail and printed newsletters

Direct mail is either addressed or unadressed. Unadressed is of course cheaper and can be targetted to specific neighbourhoods. However, your letters are very likely to find their way into the trash. Addressed direct mail may be more effective, but you will want to consider how much response you should expect. Usually direct response advertising, unless you have an established relationship, will result in less than two to three per cent response rates. This type of marketing can get expensive, but doesn't need to be, and of course you can test variations before committing significant resources. Jon Goldman at LumpyMail advocates the use of stand-out promotional items and gifts with your mailings to increase response. These could work, but again you need to consider the image and style of your business (and if you wish to go this route, you may wish to research other, potentially less expensive, suppliers).

Letters and printed newsletters for established clients or people with whom you wish to maintain a relationship may be cost-effective. The biggest challenge is maintaining discipline. You need to publish your newsletters on a reliable schedule, and you may not be able to measure results right away. You can use newsletter writing and distribution services like Construction Break (www.construction-break.com) to organize this process for you. You may find your best approach is simply to use an electronic newsletter.

Colour, paper stock, copies, distribution and more

Printed media includes many variables. You can print on high quality paper or the cheapest stock available. You can print one or two copies or many thousand. Generally, I believe it is easy to think too much about these details. Your main concern should be who is receiving your message, how often you want these individuals to receive it, and the nature of your service. Don't agonize over the details. Use stock layout services or contract with designers and publishers familiar with the industry. Remember that most office photocopiers now can produce reasonably high quality colour images at a low per-copy price. You won't want to use this to produce a slick brochure, but you may not need that for most audiences. The issue is less the media you use than the message you convey – and this relates to your clients' interests and priorities.

Chapter 14

Home and trade shows:
Discovering your clients

Do shows work?

Depending on your perspective, consumer and business-to-business trade shows are either one of the most effective marketing resources you can use or an incredible waste of time and money. In some cases, the same show can appear to be both. You spend long hours waiting for something to happen and then achieve a flurry of useful businesses or leads within minutes, which make the whole thing worthwhile.

In many ways, trade shows are like retail businesses. During show hours, you must be open for business and ready for clients who show up. Sometimes none do or those who appear at your door (or more accurately booth) are ones you would rather not see. Unlike Internet or most construction businesses where you can be relatively comfortable and rested while on standby, with the trade show you must be ready to go, no matter what happens. This is hard work.

The advantages – real connections with real people

In addition to booth rental, you need to factor in your staff costs, travel expenses (if you are going out of town), equipment and materials rentals at the show site (the show services generally gouge exhibitors with prices they would never expect to get elsewhere), and the denied opportunity to do other things because you and your employees must be on the show floor.

These costs are offset by the advantages. At the right shows, within days, you have the opportunity to connect face-to-face with many potential clients accelerating the trust building and confidence building process in the sales cycle.

As well, shows are an ideal environment for you to maintain and renew existing client relationships, gather competitive intelligence (of course your competitors will be doing the same thing about you), and for internal staff meetings and discussions in informal settings, especially if your business, like mine, has widely dispersed employees.

Qualifying your show guests

Most trade show booths are boring and most "give aways" are predictable. Almost inevitably, you'll find people visit your booth to take whatever you have for free and give little in return. In fact, many students and retired people attend shows just to pick up the trinkets and have fun gathering material for later reading or pack-rat collecting. If something is not nailed down at your table, expect it to be removed.

Then, just as a pile of students crowd into your space for your freebees, the key person you really want to meet shows up or someone you don't know, who might be a worthy prospect, arrives. If you are alone, you have to make a quick decision about how to handle things. You don't want to be disrespectful of the people who cannot do business with you, but you do want to focus on the ones who will.

The key is to have a quick strategy to qualify your visitors, asking a few straightforward questions while sharing ideas and insights with them. You want to learn more about the people you are meeting than to sell your services in the early going. The person who seems to be really interested in you could, in fact, be a competitor simply seeking to pick your brains or gather intelligence!

Gathering your leads

Many shows offer (expensive) lead retrieval systems. You may be able to purchase one of these computerized bar code readers online for significantly less, but you may also find in business-to-business shows, just inviting your prospects to provide their business card is enough. (Retirees or students won't have cards, and you can write down the information from the few key prospects who don't.)

You can offer a contest or give-away in exchange for consumers or potential clients filling in a form; sometimes these are quite elaborate, but I would keep it simple. When all the leads are gathered either at the end of each day of the show (or if the volume isn't so great, at the end of the show itself), you need to compile the data because you will want to measure the results.

Lead assignment and follow-up

Businesses have different approaches to managing the leads gathered at shows. Some centralize the lead management process or, conversely, allow sales representatives to do what they wish. Others maintain territorial systems, in which representatives are encouraged to communicate with each other and share their leads. We use a combined approach. None of our representatives have exclusivity, but they each are responsible for their own primary market areas. If another sales representative gets a lead "out of zone" at the show, he or she is expected to work co-operatively and share the lead with the person in the appropriate market area, but the initial lead is credited to the person who actually discovers it. This allows us to assess how each sales rep is performing, and encourages everyone to work on finding leads, even if they aren't in their territory.

Follow up is vital

Show experts advise that follow-up is essential. Obviously, you should fulfill any commitments you make on the show floor, either to send additional information, call for an appointment, or to add the prospect to your newsletter list. However, clearly you don't want to spend huge amounts of time on "B" or worse "C" prospects, ones that could do business with you in the future, or are simply unlikely to ever work with you. The simple solution is to do what you say you will do, and only commit at the show to doing stuff you can deliver (rather obvious, eh).

Choosing your shows

Some shows are successful, others will waste your time and budget Almost always, especially if you don't have much show experience, you should be wary of a new show or one which is untried. Visit the show yourself as a consumer and see if it matches your market objectives. If possible, you can discuss the show with non-competitive peers.

Usually the biggest and best shows stand out from the others. Few things are more frustrating than spending hour after hour complaining to your fellow exhibitors about how bad the show is – you can't leave, but you can't do any business. (If you encounter this situation, you may be able to turn lemons into lemonade by chatting with fellow exhibitors about joint ventures, lead sharing, and other initiatives where you may be able to work together in the future.)

Show cost savings techniques

You can reduce your costs and risks of show participation by seeking co-op support from your suppliers and, in some cases (subject to show guidelines) sharing your booth space with them or non-competing businesses.

A worthy approach to evaluating the show is for you to arrange with a friendly business to share their booth. You help them by reducing their staffing load, while gathering intelligence to see if your full-scale participation is worthwhile for the next scheduled show.

If you can, bring your own materials and show booth displays, complying with the show rules of course. (Note you may find real bargains for show display set-up materials on online auction sites like eBay – I paid $25.00 for a table-top set up that would have cost $500 or more new.) On-site equipment and support service rentals are expensive, but don't skimp if you need to spend the money. Remember that you are making a first impression and you want it to reflect on your business appropriately. This means if you are down-to-earth, you shouldn't put on airs, but if you are serving the high end marketplace don't look like you are running a dump.

Speaking, seminars, and tactile displays

Many shows have a conference or speaking program, and these opportunities can be useful. If you have something you think may be worthwhile, contribute. Remember that shows allow you to capture all the senses of your visitors. You can use the senses of touch, taste, and smell in the show environment and, where it is appropriate, you should do this. Bring samples; engage your visitors in the process of "feeling" your product or service, and you'll achieve greater recognition and impact.

Creativity: Some ideas for success

I asked readers of my newsletter and the Contractor Talk forums for some ideas on how to make their shows more successful, and received some intriguing suggestions.

Paul Lesieur, of Silvertree Kitchens and Bath in Minneapolis, suggested:

1. Have something of interest to make people look. Example; a stick frame home in miniature for a builder, a block of gyp-

sum for a drywall company, a sculpture made of concrete for a concrete guy.

2.   Make something new! Make your booth from materials you use, but use them differently. I made a 10′ display from maple veneered hollow core doors. Everyone one else used fabric backgrounds.

3.   Get a woman to work the show with you, the buyers are mostly women.

A plumber's show success story

Leonard Megliola, owner of Bestline Plumbing and Heating in Los Angeles, says home shows are vital to his business. Here are his observations:

This is how you steal the entire show and get everyone to come, to your booth, from one to five times.

First, if you are going to spend the time and money, to do a home show, don't do a sloppy job and come back complaining that the traffic was slow and the customers were lousy. Do it right and take the credit.

When we set up a booth, for a three day show (really two because Fridays are set-up days and don't count) we need five employees to man our booth. All our competitors turn green when they see the traffic we attract.

This is how we do it. We buy a 10 inch acrylic tube. We place the tube on a table and fill it to the top with candy. We usually buy about $500 worth of Jolly Ranch candies and we buy about $300 worth of Mickey Mouse lollipops. Every year, we buy about 300,000 very nice ink pens from China for about six cents each. We buy about 300,000 5″ x 7″ magnetic calendars, that are beautiful, for about eight cents each.

Now, here is the gimmick. People fight in line to get the Mickey Mouse lollipops, they get their hand stuck, inside the tube, trying to get them, and guess what happens? Many people keep coming back to the booth, several times, for more goodies.

We place the lollipops, ink pens, and calendars on the table. Everyone comes to our booth from one to five times. No lie. Look at the picture of our booth in the link.

The acrylic tube cost about $400. We cut a U-shaped hole at the bottom to retrieve the candy. The $1,200 we spend is peanuts compared to the return on our investment. We have sold as much as $240,000 in just a two day show and people remember us for years because of the lollipops.

At our next show, we are going to add helium balloons.

Of course, you need a few clip boards your prospects can fill out. Have several clip boards and pens on the table because people write slow and they will clog the booth. The forms should ask their name, address, phone, what type of service they are interested in, and a time to contact them.

We always offer a Home Show Special of 10 per cent. Advertise as many prices as you can. If you have average prices, write them on brochures. People love prices.

I'll tell you one more trick that attracts people. If you use the candy tube, you will not need this trick. If you don't, then this one works great. Get someone to stand on the outside of your booth and pretend that they are talking to you. This attracts customers every time. I showed this to many other vendors and they were amazed.

Here is one more trick. We had a magician come to our booth to do tricks. At times, the people were 20 deep.

One last thing; look at the age of the people at the booth. These are not children. These are the 'Money People'.

You may not wish to go as far off the wall as Leonard Megliola, but you can't argue with his success.

The conclusion: Improving your cost/value per lead

You may value the soft advantages of show participation, including maintaining client relationships and competitive intelligence, but in the end, the key number you will wish to measure is your cost and value per lead, along with the net business and profitability achieved from the show. You can set up fancy tracking systems, but we found a simple form where all salespeople list their leads, likeliness to convert, and progress is enough. Then, once a month, we ask them to update the report so by the time the next show arrives, we can total up the value and lead conversion success.

Chapter 15

Other places to advertise: Radio, television, billboards, and your truck

Breaking through the clutter: Can you?

You probably receive more than your share of calls from media salespeople offering one promotional opportunity or another. You may be tempted to "bite," but use some common sense: Advertising can be expensive, and few media outlets will guarantee results. (If a media sales representative really guarantees that there are no up-front fees and you will only pay if your advertising is successful, let me know.)

Radio and television

Consultant Michael Stone says most contractors don't achieve great results – unless they are well established – with radio and television advertising. Low budget cable television ads may be inexpensive, but the response rate is usually so low that you won't receive proper return on your investment. Conversely, in Columbus, Ohio, Mike Feazel of Feazel Roofing says he spends upwards of $200,000 a year on radio advertising and receives about a third of his business that way. Feazel says if you wish to emulate his example, you should be prepared to budget at least $20,000 a month for several months, a clear entry barrier for most contractors.

Billboards and signs

Billboards are probably not a wise investment for most contractors; you need the right location and it is unlikely enough passing traffic will be interested in your services. However, job site and vehicle signs are important. Consider creative "wrap" messages on your trucks to attract attention, especially at job sites, where referrals are possible. You can place "take one" brochures and business card drop-boxes on your trailers.

Consider offering clients a small discount in exchange for the right to post signs at job sites. You will receive calls and they will be inexpensive leads.

Alternative media and promotional items

Logo pens, coasters, direct mail pieces shaped as coconuts or garbage pails, name-embossed welcome mats, and other gimmicks might work, in the right circumstances. You can also spend a small fortune on promotional goodies to find they gather dust or generate no leads all. If you wish to use these resources, go softly, test, and look carefully at what your clients enjoy. If you see an interesting promotional item in your best clients' office or home, ask about it and see if you can can replicate the idea elsewhere.

Place a sticker near your completed work – say the furnace or air conditioning unit – with your maintenance service and call-back number. It costs just a few cents, but your clients will easily find the number when they need you the most.

Combine advertising methods for the best results

You should combine several marketing and advertising approaches simultaneously. Focus the marketing on your ideal potential clients and let them know about through a variety of media.

However, remember that your best marketing message is in the service you deliver. Your advertising will be wasted if your receptionist is insensitive, you fail to return calls promptly and your work is poor. Nothing can destroy your brand more quickly than inconsistent over-promising and under-delivering.

Chapter 16

Media publicity: Magnifying positive word of mouth for your business

The publicity home run

You will hit a marketing home run if your local newspaper or television station profiles your business on its news program in a positive feature article. Conversely, you could be forced into bankruptcy if the opposite happens. Media publicity, of course, is a two-edged sword. It magnifies everything. If you have a great reputation and positive word of mouth spreads, you'll multiply the results with positive publicity. The reverse applies if your story is negative.

The big challenge with publicity is that you cannot control its timing and results. With one special exception to be discussed later, you can't expect the news program producer or publisher to distribute your story, exactly as provided, on your schedule. Nor, in most cases, will your relationship as an advertiser with the publisher influence or control the news coverage.

Publicity's return on investment is usually worthwhile

However, you can still manage and plan the publicity-seeking process and here the reward for your input effort will far exceed the cost. Say, you have a $100,000 advertising and promotion budget. Would you achieve greater results by spending the money on print and Internet ads or by hiring or contracting with a competent media relations employee or consultant? I expect your return on investment would be significantly higher if you invested in the media relations process rather than the advertising. (If your advertising is effective, then you may find allocating additional funds for publicity initiatives will enhance your advertising's effectiveness.)

If your business is smaller, you will need to attract the publicity yourself, but again, your reward for effort will be potentially far greater than rushing around like a sparrow, submitting one public tender bid after another, hoping something succeeds.

Publicity creates credibility

The reason solid media publicity is so valuable is its helpful impact on your credibility, trust, and therefore your brand. Positive publicity is like great word of mouth, magnified by the reputation and distribution of the media outlet generating the news. With a credible media presence, you will find doors will open that you didn't know exist, and existing clients will be more willing to enthusiastically refer and support your business.

Of course, the converse also applies if you are caught up in scandal or bad news, such as safety-related job site deaths, fines or civil/criminal penalties associated with your projects, or consumer complaints of poor service or work quality. You need to be prepared with crisis contingency plans, a set of protocols and rules designed to minimize the damage and (in some cases) restore your business reputation quickly. You won't have the resources for this level of formal planning if you are small but you should always be aware of the rules of the game. Then, if a crisis occurs, you will be able to reduce the damage of negative publicity.

Make sure everything is in order first

Be sure all is in order at your business before you seek media attention. You certainly don't want publicity if your employees are violating ethical guidelines, if your site crews are so undisciplined that they don't care about safety, and your client service is so sloppy that people are complaining.

Publicity consultants

Public/media relations consultants and specialists vary greatly in competence. Large known PR agencies may attract you with their best rainmakers, but then assign a junior who doesn't know how to think creatively and is constrained to recommend ineffective, bland, and boring strategies.

You can connect with peers in your community and trade association for guidance. If one of your best clients or suppliers is achieving great media relations success, find out how they are doing it. Through references from your trade associations, you may find colleagues in other cities who have achieved great results. Often you can borrow the great ideas elsewhere and apply them in your own community, where they will appear to be new.

In most communities, community colleges have publicity/media relations programs. Students can be inexpensive, but their work quality will be uneven. You may connect with media relations specialists and consultants through your community service and non-profit marketing contributions (a great way to gain some publicity for yourself).

I'll be happy to exchange email ideas with you about publicity options relevant to you at no charge, and consult with you by phone for an hourly fee in greater detail if you prefer. You can reach me directly at buckshon@cnrgp.com. For my free e-book, *The Art and Science of Publicity*, email publicity@cnrgp.com.

Chapter 16

Your publicity building blocks

The news release

This is the standard publicity resource. You write a news style article, usually about 500 to 750 words, with a strong but dispassionate message and succinct, attention-grabbing headline. Don't use phoney superlatives, make unsubstantiated promotional claims or puff your story with clichés. You need to be newsworthy, and tell your story so that it is interesting to your readers.

NOTE: The newsworthiness threshold has declined with the Internet era. Now many seemingly minor issues can justify a news release. Fed through Internet news service providers, these announcements can boost your search engine rankings.

Media lists and news release dissemination services

You can compile your own media list, but you will find it easier to use the news dissemination services such as Canada News Wire or PR Newswire. You pay a fee, but can be sure your news release will be distributed. Your news release will find its way on to websites and in some cases, if your story is truly compelling, you will receive some coverage in other print and electronic media. You can also use free Internet services.

Third party power and relationships

The strongest and most powerful media management techniques occur when you develop creative strategies behind the scenes, especially when you relate your organization to community service or non-profit activities. Obviously I'm not suggesting you fake who you really are – that could lead to a true public relations disaster – but if you can affiliate with causes, issues, and passionate people who care about these matters, you'll likely get more press. The reason is that reporters have a natural bias in favour of non-profit groups; they (and their publishers) believe businesses should pay for advertising.

Drama, excitement, creativity and fun

Co-ordinate exciting events or activities that reflect your brand / values and serve your community. You can also, to a lesser extent, piggyback on other community activities. Many construction industry organizations participate in Habitat for Humanity projects: These contributions are useful and rewarding but will generate you far less publicity than your success in winning the contract to demolish your county's crack houses, receiving permission to invite television crews and the local newspaper to a demolition site.

Stunts (wild, off the wall, and dramatic events) sometimes work, but be careful as the publicity can backfire on you. Also, consider whether these activities fit your brand and marketing position: If you are a conservative, thoughtful and reliable industry practitioner, having your company president dressed up as "Joe the Plumber" at a public bond hearing or financing meeting might gain you some local publicity – but will you attract any useful new business?

Nevertheless, don't be afraid to take risks and to speak out on controversial topics. Just make sure your point of view reflects both your own values and those of your current and potential clients.

Seed publicity and magnifying results

Once you have received publicity in one media outlet, you can enhance the process by sharing the news and drawing in other media organizations. For example, if you are profiled positively in the local business newspaper, you may find you can send a note to your daily newspaper, suggesting to them that they can make the story relevant to their readers. Even easier, you can take the daily newspaper's article and send a copy with cover note to community weeklies and trade journals (especially of your potential clients). You can also apply the same principles to the electronic media.

Your reputation as an expert

Publicity turns you into the expert. Make yourself available to reporters as a source of information about your speciality. This is especially useful if your services relate to topics that are newsworthy, but often personal or confidential. (If you, for example, specialize in insolvencies or insurance restoration work, your clients probably won't wish to receive too much direct publicity. In fact, you may be sworn to confidentiality about the circumstances — but you certainly can speak on economic trends and how people and businesses can avoid problems.)

You will achieve media guru status by communicating well and reliably. Often you can get started by sending brief notes to reporters and journalists. You may also find it worthwhile to send your informative newsletter, individually addressed, to reporters and editors as well as current and potential clients. (See the the next chapter for newsletter ideas).

Returning calls and communicating with journalists

You should respond quickly and authoritatively to journalists who call. Interrupt almost anything to respond to a media inquiry or return call from your news releases or announcements. (Accordingly, plan your schedule to allow time to respond when you issue news releases or announcements.) When you speak with the press, be absolutely truthful. If you don't know the answer, it is far better to admit it than to fake it. You can offer to obtain the information and to call back. Be sure to follow up in time to meet all deadlines.

Some businesses have strict rules about who should talk with journalists and how to handle these calls. There are good reasons for these rules. Uninformed and inexperienced employees can blurt out things that could damage your reputation. Of course, conversely, if your business operates with an open and responsive culture, you may find your employees' spontaneous initiatives create incredibly positive publicity. For example, not knowing your client is a journalist, an employee treats her with such great respect and positive service that she enthuses about your business in a news article.

The more you need to control what your employees say to the media, the harder you need to work on your internal practices and policies to make things right. You can simply encourage your employees to respectfully refer the media calls to your designated media spokesperson or yourself. Most journalists will accept this as a common-sense business procedure.

Articles, speeches and books

You can create publicity for yourself by writing articles and stories, giving speeches and writing books on the topics of interest and relevance to your business. These ideas are discussed in greater detail in the next chapter.

Hiring experts to help

If you don't have these talents, you can learn them, or hire experts to help you. Many people, for example, work with professional writers to produce books and articles, which are ghost-written in your name. You spend time with the writer, make suggestions about what works best, and the writer then crafts the words to reflect your voice. You, of course, still need to be actively engaged in these processes, and you should expect to pay significant fees for this work (although if you are on a low budget you can often find a student or part-time writer willing to work for below-market prices.)

Combining publicity resources

Note these resources can be combined, magnifying the results you achieve for your time investment. You take the articles you write for various publications, meld them into client newsletter pieces, adapt your thoughts and phraseology to speeches, and combine all the pieces into a book, which you then promote with publicity and effective media relations practices. All of these initiatives ultimately improve your personal credibility and reputation, and create more demand and interest in your services, as they enhance your brand.

New media – social networking

Services such as Twitter, Facebook and LinkedIn as well as more specialized Internet forums and sites such as Contractor Talk and Remodel Crazy provide incredibly rich publicity opportunities for you. This is because many media outlets monitor the Internet sites closely for trends and issues of relevance, and if you are seen as an expert on these sites, you will gain attention. I discuss these resources more closely in the chapter on online marketing. In some cases, media publicity initiatives have been set up on these forums. In one case, a few years ago, a frequent-fliers group to which I belonged to created a public firestorm against a major airline on an Internet forum. We knew key journalists were watching.

Awards and competitions

If your association or community group has an award or competition for any category relevant to your business, you should always consider either nominating your business or encouraging your clients to nominate you. Then take the effort in preparing the submission as well as you would your best RFP proposals. The most effective awards occur when they are validated by the media.

For example, our publications have an annual Readers' Choice competition. Our rules for submitting nominations and selecting finalists are simple. Anyone qualified can nominate themselves or the organizations they choose. We'll announce the winners from the organizations that receive the most votes. Frankly, we expect some campaigning here and don't mind. Winners are recognized with positive publicity and need not spend a cent.

You will find competitions within trade associations, public service groups, Chambers of Commerce, and so on. Enter them.

Paid competitions

Some commercial businesses and organizations set up competitions and make money from the fees and entries. You need to decide if this is a worthwhile expense. The advantages can be similar to "advertorials" described below. You may be able to control the results to some extent, and the contest organizer may have achieved enough credibility that the investment is worthwhile. However, I would generally avoid paying fees to enter competitions unless they are operated by reputable community and non-profit groups.

Measuring your results

Unlike conventional advertising, it is hard to plan and project your results for media relations and publicity. You simply don't know in advance what will work, and what won't. The indirect benefits of solid positive publicity are truly hard to measure. Consider for example what happens when you appear as an expert on a local news program. Someone who needs your services might call you right away. You may also find one of your current clients shares the news with a friend that you really are as good as you sounded on television. You will receive a referral call but you don't know why it happened.

You can measure the results in the number of articles published, the responses attributed directly to the publicity, and so on, but I would advocate you measure results by what you actually can control: Your response time in returning media calls, the number of articles you are able to publish in relevant trade journals, and so on.

A special note about advertorials

You will, from time to time, be invited to have your business profiled in an editorial-style feature for which you are expected to pay a fee. Publications and electronic media outlets offer these services because they are easier to sell and often more effective than conventional advertising. They also give you control over timing and the message you wish to convey, something impossible with regular media publicity.

Our business earns most of its revenue from "advertorials," packaged as special features. We work with your suppliers to encourage them to purchase supporting advertisements for your business. If we attain enough revenue from the sales, we write the feature article without requiring you to spend any of your own money. This can result in 3-, 4-, or even 8- to 16-page features.

These advertorials are effective because they are (a) written by trained journalists; (b) designed to be credible in style and content; and (c) they are not budget breakers. As well, your suppliers receive value: they achieve recognition as being good enough to do business with you (thus they are also good enough for other clients). We practice what we preach and provide service levels far beyond the basics: Anyone who advertises is our client and is treated with respect.

Other publications offer similar services. You need to decide how and when to use these resources. Clearly, you don't want to hit up your suppliers too often – unless you wish them to add the cost of all the publicity to their invoices to you! Also, you need to consider the likely long-term value of advertorial-type publicity within your market and community.

If you have $100,000 to spend on publicity and advertising, you will get much better results by spending $20,000 on media relationships and business development, than by spending everything on advertising. You might want to free some of the remaining $80,000 for advertorials in selected media.

If your budget is smaller, you may find an investment of $1,500 in a paid feature, such as our *Design and Construction Report*, is worth every cent because you can use this to enhance client interest and attract other media attention. For more information, email publicity@cnrgp.com.

Chapter 18

Articles, newsletters, speeches and books: The path to high-powered marketing credibility

If you enjoy and are good at writing, you'll love the ideas in this chapter. I do. You may recall that one of this book's primary ideas is that your marketing success depends primarily on doing what you enjoy the most and relating your passions and talents to your clients.

You don't have to be a writing genius to communicate effectively if you have knowledge, passion, and sincerity on your side. Write what you feel and pass the words on to someone else for cleaning up and editing. You can hire ghost writers.

Articles – the building block

Articles, either printed or on the Internet (many blog entries can be articles) are expressions around a single theme. These can often be built through formulas, where you mix and match certain fundamental writing concepts to achieve the best results. Ford Harding in his book *Rain Making: The Professional's Guide to Attracting New Clients* suggests some of these formulas, which I adapted within a day to produce my *Seven Tips for Construction Marketing Success*, which you can easily discover by searching on Google for "construction marketing."

Be familiar with the publications

You should be familiar with the publications where your articles will appear. In the early stages of your writing career, this will likely be relevant association journals and trade publications. Often these journals and newsletters struggle to find relevant content to fill their pages. So if you have something useful, they will likely publish it. Introduce yourself with an email or note to the editor.

Articles should generally be reasonably short, about 750 to 1,000 words (two to three type-written double-spaced pages) unless the journal wishes longer submissions.

Newsletters – Keeping in touch

Newsletters allow you to keep in touch with prospective, current and former clients. They are also inexpensive, virtually free if you publish them electronically. You can also also publish printed newsletters with your office colour photocopier. If you wish to convey a high-quality image – essential, if you are an architect – consider contracting with a printer who will ensure the newsletter reflects your standards.

Some services, such as David "Woody" Wood's Construction Break, provide newsletter writing and production services. For a modest fee, they'll co-ordinate the writing of company-specific content with stock material designed to brighten your readers' days.

These services also remove one of the biggest problems with newsletter projects: You start them, and then stop, because of the work/time involved and your perception that immediate results are not overwhelming. With the external services, which have set production schedules, you won't need to agonize over completing the job (and you'll be able to include it in your annual marketing budget).

Electronic newsletter guidelines

Never distribute a newsletter primarily containing advertising and self-promotional news. Also, never send the newsletter to people who don't want it or don't know you (unless there is absolutely no selling and lots of real giving, and even then, only with real caution). You do not want to distribute spam. Any business you receive will be more than offset by the negative image and backlash you create.

Make it easy for readers to cancel and accept these requests gracefully.

Building the template

Several online services can manage your e-list and distribute newsletters. I've been using Constant Contact (www.constant-contact.com). You can combine Constant Contact email capacities with archival, polling and survey resources, adding to your knowledge and encouraging reader interaction. Other email services can be equally effective.

You can use templates or, if you wish, a professional web designer can upload a customized design.

You can design and mail different newsletters to different market segments. This makes sense at the highest level of marketing, but if you are like me, you will probably want to get started with one newsletter and not worry too much about segmenting separate newsletters for different client groups. However, as your business grows, consider the diverse interests of your readers and develop newsletters for each group or community.

Giving is great

Sure, you can use your newsletters to tell readers about your accomplishments, announce services, new hires, and the like. However, your newsletter will have greatest value when you focus on sharing valuable information readers can use even if they don't decide to do business with you. The reciprocity principle applies. While some readers will only take your information and not return anything, others will return the favour. You will attract and retain new business.

Speeches – achieving a high profile within your community

Successful article and newsletter writing leads to the next stage in communication/persuasion: speeches and public appearances. You can speak at community functions and events, association meetings, and the like. You should combine passion for your topic and respect for your audience, and you need both technical speaking skills and self-confidence to succeed in front of the crowd. These seemingly huge barriers explain why speech-giving is such a powerful marketing tool. Few are willing to try, and even fewer speak really well.

You can practice at Toastmasters International meetings (there are chapters in virtually every community, see www.toastmasters.org for more information).

Speeches are incredibly powerful for networking. A great speech guarantees you credibility, and since you are in the room, people can approach you to ask you questions and begin a business-building relationship.

Writing the book about book writing

You are reading my first book, written after a life-time of professional writing. If you think giving speech is a huge challenge, book writing is even more daunting the first time around. You obviously need discipline (and a great editor) to write a book. Everyone has their own approach, but I found I could get the job done by waking up at 5:00 a.m. every day for a several months, and writing about 90 minutes to two hours. I had no excuses to miss my writing time and I know that I write best in the early morning, in any case.

I also called on a writing coach. Several are available, but Cindy Shearer (www.cindyshearer.com) based in the San Francisco area, helped immensely in framing my understanding, setting the schedule, and reminding me of what is important. You'll also need a great editor. (I'm lucky in that regard. My wife Vivian is a professional writer and editor.)

Even with this support, the book writing project which I had expected to take only a few months, took more than a year to complete. You can do it faster, but you'll need to overcome distractions to successfully complete the project.

Getting published

You can either seek an outside publisher or do it yourself. Self-publishing through print-on-demand allows you to produce a high quality book at modest cost. This is not the vanity press of previous generations, where you would submit your manuscript to a "we publish anything" service, that would flatter you by telling you how great you are and how they will publish the book for a (high) fee. The stigma against self-publishing has disappeared, especially for professional advice and how-to books.

However, if you self-publish, you should realize that you have an uphill battle in marketing and distributing your book. Before you start, you should listen carefully to anyone who offers constructive criticism (and you should seek it out). You don't want to publish an embarrassing and costly dud.

Finding a publisher

You may find third-party publishers interested in your ideas. For example, the Society for Marketing Professional Services (SMPS) has a publishing division which may help you complete the process and get to print. Don't expect to be published initially by the major commercial publishers – that would be kind of like walking off the street and being accepted into the National Football League.

Print on demand services

Many self publishers use online print-on demand services such as LuLu (www.lulu.com). These businesses will guide you through the process of turning your manuscript into a book, then make it available for you either online or in print, only producing copies when you receive orders.

Their biggest problems are add-on and extra fees, which will make the "unit cost" of your final printed product relatively high. If you have publishing experience or a designer familiar with the publishing process, use a wholesale service, Lightning Source (www.lighteningsource.com). You will need to work with a professional designer. You can request a quotation from our designer, Raymond Leveille, at raymond@memoproductions.com

Audio and video presentations

If you are more visually than word oriented, you can also consider the options in producing videos, "webinars" and audio messages for iPod distribution. Personally, I shudder at the thought of using these resources, but you can now produce at modest cost a live web video program on a regular schedule with your simple computer-based video camera and access to a streaming video service. Many marketers have discovered webinars are effective in building relationships, attracting audience participation, and building marketing credibility.

Measuring your results

You will find acceptance of your article is the first stage of the process – but will you see much from it immediately? It depends. When I sent in my first article to Randy Pollack at the *SMPS Marketer* about blogging, I thought I'd notice a significant increase in the number of visitors to my blog when the 6,500 readers of the association publication read the piece. Nothing happened. However, my writing was good enough that Randy accepted my second proposal, and then invited me to join *The Marketer's* editorial committee. This certainly has helped my networking.

You will also find another cost- and time-saving resource as you write. You can recycle the materials into your blog, newsletters, and (where appropriate) marketing materials for prospective new clients.

The writing also becomes your speech content and sometimes you can recycle virtually the same article in different (non-competitive) magazines and newsletters. In other words, each group of words you produce has many functions.

Write and communicate through speeches, electronic newsletters, video presentations and books. Your credibility will increase. If you have the talent, inclination and drive to communicate your message, these resources should rank high on your marketing priority list.

Chapter 19

RFPs and public bids: The world is fair, but only if you know the rules

How to stack the deck in your favour

A general contractor in a mid-west state, which must remain nameless, has great luck in winning bids with a local hospital authority. All of the bidding opportunities are open, advertised publicly, and the bidding rules are defined so that the low price is really the only thing that counts. For some reason, the general contractor is always "low," and wins job after job.

The story isn't quite what it seems. The contracting business president told me in an off-the-record interview that the reason his company wins and achieves profitability on all the low bids is that his estimators and the hospital purchasers have made an agreement to be deliberately vague in certain aspects about the scope of work for advertised projects. They also agree that this "confusion" will result in change orders, which can be charged properly and profitably going forward.

Ethics and the real world

Now, you are absolutely correct in observing that this practice is unethical and unfair to everyone else and invites corruption allegations. However, there are ethically valid reasons the hospital and contractor are in cahoots. The contractor has reliably done great work over the years in the hospital and has built solid and warm relationships with the hospital administration and staff. Rather than risking the unknown, the hospital and contractor agree to manipulate the system.

This sort of thing happens on a truly large percentage of jobs which are set out for public competition. We will never find official statistics on how many bids are "wired" in favour of one contractor (or engineer, architect or consultant) or another, but old hands in the industry rarely chase projects which they know they will lose. They've been tipped off ahead of time, one way or another, that they are the selected winners, and they know the work is there for the asking.

The Brooks Act and its implications

This predetermined aspect of the bidding process is magnified now that public and government agencies are able to incorporate qualitative as well as quantitative measurements in their assessment. If points are assessed for subjective issues, who do you think will win? The stranger, who arrives out of the blue with the "low price" or the contractor, who has done similar work with the clients for years.

In the U.S., the qualitative and relationship-focussed approach to architectural and engineering design procurement is set out by law. Federal and many state procurement rules under the 35-year old Brooks Act specifically remove price from primary consideration for architectural and engineering design proposals – subjective qualifications, largely defined by previous relationships, underlie the selection process. (See page 159 for more Brooks Act information).

You want to be an insider rather than outsider

The more I learn about effective bid preparation and proposals, the more I realize there really are two worlds out there: insiders and outsiders. You want to be an insider. It is a much more fun place to be.

Take for example a recent situation where we were invited to submit a proposal on a new publication for local renovators, sponsored by the local home builders association. I can't go into all the details here, because this story is too close to home, but I knew for certain that this situation indeed represented a "wired" bid. You will generally know without question when you are on the inside.

Your go or no go decision

Since clearly we had earned the inside-track opportunity, my challenge was to decide whether to go or not to go for the project, a key decision in any bidding situation. Here, the problem was that the work was outside my primary business scope of work and responsibility/ expertise. This is usually a warning sign to stay away. You don't chase projects for which you lack competence, experience or market focus, and projects that distract you from your priorities, even if the projects themselves, are on the surface, tempting.

Nevertheless, the person making the call had been a great client for other work within our scope, so I set out to solve the problem. I phoned a colleague who had expertise within the area of the proposed project. He called someone he knew with retail rather than trade publishing experience. Within a few days, we were ready for our initial planning meeting.

We crunched numbers, reviewed the project parameters (I showed my new partners on an eyes-only basis that indeed I had special access to the opportunity), and decided we would tackle the project.

Team building the natural way

Note how I assembled the team here. No public consultation with wide-ranging research, no hours of evaluating competing options, and so on. I knew who to call and the person I knew, knew others. The entire team selection process took just a few hours total — and for my own time, just one lunch.

Soon, I received a call from the project proponent. He said the association would need to advertise it publicly in a notice to members. Fair enough, I thought. An obscure posting one time on an association e-mail would not present too much competition.

Facing public competition (when the game is stacked in your favour)

Then something surprising happened. After the single advertisement, the association office received a flood of inquiries. In fact, five competing organizations appeared out of the woodwork to bid the job. We were stunned. Our client's project co-ordinator said everyone would need to be treated fairly, and my team didn't object. However, this win would not be a slam-dunk, we knew now. Still, we had the original inside track. We discussed whether we needed to sharpen our pencils and bring in a lower bid. "No," I argued. "We should not do the job if we cannot make a reasonable profit. We'll deliver the best project, so let's deliver the best proposal."

My partners, experienced in design and sales, helped assemble the proposal documentation (I did much of the writing). We then bound and prepared copies of the eight-page booklet. We had a pre-presentation meeting to go over our strategies and decided to show up at the association offices about 30 minutes early to avoid any risk of arriving late.

In the hallway at the association offices, the person who had invited me to make the original proposal greeted us warmly. At least two of the opposing candidates had failed to show up for the presentation invitation. Then we watched as the other two candidates went into the room, one after another. One had travelled almost an hour from out of town. She had a computerized marketing presentation, which she was to demonstrate on a portable display screen. She started it up in the waiting room and it looked like she was about to use the same presentation she gave everywhere else.

Then another candidate, the person who originally presented a proposal (and who thought he had the job in the bag) sauntered into the room dressed in jeans, carrying binders of research material. Huh, we thought, sitting outside, waiting. Does this guy not know that we've been specifically invited to bid the job and win it so he couldn't get it?

The insider's welcome

Our turn arrived. We entered the room, materials in hand, and spent thirty minutes answering questions, including a key one to ensure we would hold our prices and margins intact. No, we could not guarantee significant cash benefits or repayments to the committee, but we could certainly deliver a project that would create great value. When we finished our presentation, 14 committee members applauded. Not surprisingly, we won the job.

What happened here? How much marketing time and effort did we need to expend to engage in a project potentially worth hundreds of thousands of dollars each year? Seems it was ours for the asking. Clearly, this is not the hard and difficult marketing you would expect for a big project, but this is the world we live in.

Remember this important point: Projects are won on merit, but merit is defined more by your relationships and reputation with the project owners and decision-makers than by your price. They are "wired."

How you can 'wire' relations and projects in your favour

Read the book, *Wired! How to Crawl Inside Your Client's Mind for Success in Business Development* by David Stone for insights. Stone observes that you must have a great relationship in place with your potential client before you engage in the expensive and challenging process of responding to an RFP. You need clear "go — no go" rules and then you need to stick to them in making your decisions about when to pursue a job and when to skip the public proposal.

Stone also points out that the actual RFP stage is generally not the place to be trying to build relationships. In other words, it is rarely wise to submit a proposal on a project wired for someone else, hoping you will develop connections that will dazzle the selection team and result in your being chosen for future projects. The incumbents have a major advantage. They can parlay the intelligence about your excellent proposals into improvements at their end and always stay a step ahead of you. And they generally will.

Finding your way into the picture

You need another way to get into the picture. This can be as crass as hiring a project manager trusted by the client from another firm (being sure, of course, that you are really hiring the right person, not someone the opponent wishes to ditch, and the employee is not bound by non-compete covenants!) Less risky and more natural, is to build relationships and connections with your potential future clients on neutral grounds, such as association events and committees. As you build the trust, you may receive a tip-off about a real opportunity for a project that you really have a chance of winning.

Note this relationship building is generally (on one level) a really long-term thing. By the time the project reaches the stage of public announcement, you are too late if you don't already have a connection. You can of course use leads services and public announcements for clues. You will learn who is putting projects into the pipeline and perhaps obtain some key budget information. You can also track previous projects from the potential client and learn about the competitor who is winning the work. Then you can decide if you want to devote the effort and energy to persue the file, or you wish, to leave it to others.

How to use your association network effectively

Many experienced Society for Marketing Professional Services (SMPS) members say their network is helpful in discovering and winning opportunities. For example, say you are a local contractor in a mid-sized U.S. city with the opportunity to bid on a public aquarium. You have much experience and great connections with the local authorities, but you know very little about aquarium buildings. So you connect, through your association contacts, the contractor(s) who have done this type of work in other cities. You (if all goes well), know and trust your colleagues. You can then prepare a joint venture proposal.

Magnifying your success opportunities

Here, your chances of success are magnified. The outside specialist contractor may well know the people working on your local aquarium project – after all, they belong to the same aquarium trade associations and learning groups. Meanwhile, you have the local connections and expertise, including a solid network of reliable subtrades and suppliers. Whose proposal is likely to come first?

Soon, with rare exceptions, you'll almost instinctively know which projects to pursue and which ones to avoid. You'll find the ones where you have real connections are an almost sure thing. Develop and observe your go-no-go rules. Then, when it is time to "go," go all out. You will win profitable work. Do a great job, maintaining wonderful relationships all along, and you'll win even more work. This is how things work in the real world.

Chapter 20

About the Brooks Act

From the Construction Marketing Ideas *blog, September 2008*

The Brooks Act — who you know and what you know

One of this blog's readers sent me an email with a simple question: "Do you know about the Brooks Act?" It is perhaps the most important element in considering who wins architectural and engineering projects at the federal level and in many states. It creates a major barrier to entry for outsiders and a real competitive advantage and power-base for design firms with solid Washington connections and relationships.

I discovered this "old" (2002) reference to the Brooks Act on the American Society of Civil Engineers site. If you are thinking of competing for federal work as new infrastructure funds are available, read it carefully.

Brooks A/E Act Turns 30

This week marks the 30th Anniversary of the Brooks A/E Act, mandating the use of Qualifications Based Selection (QBS) for federal procurement of A/E design services. Rep. Jack Brooks (D-TX) introduced the Architect-Engineer Selection Act after a GAO report pointed out that there was no statutory basis for use of the QBS method of selection. The bill was signed into law on October 27, 1972 (Public Law 92-582).

Congress later expanded the act to include surveying and mapping as well as architecture and engineering services. Since 1972 the QBS method of procurement has been extended to include highway, mass transit and airport grant programs as well as prime and subcontracts under the Superfund program. In 1988, Congress amended the Brooks Act and supplied a new definition of covered services.

The Brooks Act, along with the ABA Model Procurement Code for State and Local Government, has set the model for procurement acts in over 35 states.

Implications for your business

Clearly, relationships and experience are vital if you wish to win business in the design aspects of federal and much state work. (The Brooks Act doesn't apply for contractors and trades, so price can still be a vital component here, but many federal departments still include experience qualifications within their evaluation criteria.)

If you are just starting out and think this is unfair, consider the alternative. In Ontario, Canada, because of industry lobbying for a transparent and open system, any contractor meeting basic qualifications could submit an application to be a "vendor of record" for provincial building work.

Suddenly, upwards of 200 contractors began receiving notifications of projects. In some cases, 50 or more showed up for site visits, and most of these applicants submitted bids. You can imagine how low the lowest bid could be in these circumstances, and how much wasted time and energy everyone else endured, only to lose the job to a business that will earn little if anything, for their work.

Do you really want the world to be this "fair"?

Chapter 21

Leads services: How to choose and use them for profitable results

Finding your match

Should leads services be part of your marketing picture?

The simple answer: It depends. If you expect leads services will take you directly to profitable projects, you will be disappointed. However, if your expectations are realistic and you use the services in a highly disciplined manner, you may find their fees to be reasonable.

Within non-residential markets, two giant lead services compete, McGraw-Hill Construction (The McGraw-Hill Companies, Inc.) and Reed Construction Data (part of Reed Elsevier plc Group.) They have several smaller competitors focusing on regional or local markets.

Online leads services

Competitors such as BidClerk charge much lower monthly fees, but they don't always gather all the nuances of local projects available from the traditional services.

In the residential market, services such as Servicemagic gather consumer-focused leads online by inviting homeowners to register their interest. The services then resell the leads to contractors.

The leads services love-hate relationship

You most likely have a love-hate relationship with leads services. In some cases, you receive exactly what you want, useful leads for real business. Unlike conventional paid advertising, your results are tangible and immediate, and you can go to work right away to convert the leads into business.

Unfortunately, leads services are not perfect. They often sell the same information to several competitors, diluting the leads' value. Once the project is "open for bidding" you must be prepared to fight against others who may have entrenched relationships. In many cases, the project is already "wired" for another business, and you don't know it. Leads services may provide information about people who lack interest in your service or are cheapskates.

The run-around

Many contractors complain on Internet forums such as Contractor Talk that the leads services rarely co-operate in refunding or replacing invalid leads. The complainers often fail to understand what the services can and cannot do.

You need to decide if the cost per lead is worthwhile. In many cases, it is. But watch your back – the competition is just behind you (if they haven't reached your potential client first.)

Market research

Leads services are great sources of data you can use to strategically plan marketing initiatives.

Say, for example, you are interested in working on hospital renovations within your state. You have your own network of contacts and associates, possibly gleaned from previous experience, vendors and suppliers, and relevant associations. Leads service reports provide additional data. You can uncover names of architects, engineers and other professionals who are preparing plans and you can discover sub trades and general contractors. You may learn about projects that could require your services later.

You can use this information to make connections, track your competitors and plan your strategy.

Figuring out where to build your relationships

You can use this information for relationship-building. For example, consider sharing information from the leads service with someone in your network who might benefit from the knowledge. This creates much good-will and encourages reciprocation.

For consumer-oriented services, learn which neighbourhoods provide the most useful leads and develop your own marketing strategies to follow up and find the leads without the services. You can also share the leads information with allied trades and professionals. They will return the favour.

Leads service guidelines

Here are some leads service guidelines:

- Give the service enough time to prove its value (at least three months) but don't tie yourself down to a long-term contract to reduce your per-lead cost until you are sure the leads are good.
- For consumer leads, review postings on forums such as Contractor Talk. You will learn about their pitfalls and pluses.
- Consider construction association and building exchange services. You may use physical or electronic plans rooms to review project documentation.
- Beware of leads services representatives who use hard-selling tactics, especially telemarketers. Effective services attract and retain loyal clients. Check with your peers in non-competitive markets.

Measure your results

Measure and track your leads service results. You should know your cost per lead, conversion rate and the value of business generated per lead. You can input this information into your annual budget to effectively plan your marketing strategies.

Conclusion

Putting it all together:
Your passions and opportunities

Surviving (thriving) during the recession

In the months I've been writing this book (late 2008 and 2009), the world has changed. The U.S. elected a new president as the economy declined, with serious negative portents for the construction industry as new architectural bookings and initiatives declined to the lowest in decades.

My business experienced the usual early-recession profitability "bump" as contractors and suppliers, seeing their order-book emptying, decided to advertise. Not surprisingly, this didn't continue for too long: Advertising at the early stages of a recession is generally ineffective and a serious cash drain.

We soon felt the pinch, and our own growth ambitions suddenly turned into a survival exercise. Fortunately, I've lived through hard times before and know how roll up my sleeves, get to work, and accept responsibility. As the recession evolved and our skills developed, we began adapting and developing new business models, including exciting electronic pushing initiatives. For example, we launched the *Design and Construction Report* (www.dcnreport.com) as an online magazine in co-operation with the Design and Construction Network, established in early 2009).

"Diet pill" solutions don't work

We do our best to counsel our advertisers: The minute anyone plunks down several hundred dollars for an advertisement, they are given my telephone number and email address, and I'll share practical and inexpensive construction marketing ideas with them. We listen to clients' concerns and if they are experiencing a business crisis, we'll do whatever we can to guide them out of their mess.

I don't have magic one-size-fits-all "diet-pill" solutions for you, and anyone with quick fixes is probably scamming you. However, you can create your own luck and opportunities through passion, self-respect, an open mind and creativity.

Recession and revival – Applying the lessons

Recently, my phone and email have been ringing and pinging with intriguing opportunities, largely built on our successful brand revitalization (which correlates highly to our emphasis on giving value rather than selling stuff). We are parlaying these opportunities into new relationships along with the restoration and growth of old ties.

For example, our effort to restart *Washington Construction News* in the winter of 2009 appeared initially to falter as the recession dug into the economy. Nevertheless, we found a way to complete the circle.

In 2000 our original Washington launch seemed to be an audacious endeavour. What business does a Canadian have establishing a construction publication in the U.S. capital's metropolitan area? The major construction industry publishers, with branches and locations throughout the U.S., had left the Washington D.C. area market unoccupied.

Starting on a shoestring

I started the business on a shoestring, recruiting our initial publishers and editorial employees through seat-of-the-pants methods (we hadn't learned our recruiting and hiring systems yet), and the business took off, with incredible results, with our largest ever single issue in true net revenue published in September, 2001.

You know what happened that month (we sold our ads for the issue in August).

Through the post-2001 economic crunch and then the seeming rebound in the U.S. economy in the middle of the decade, my business started a painful and agonizing economic collapse. I blamed several reasons, including shifting currency values and the faulty assumption that, because the construction economy was then doing very well, few needed to promote their business or advertise.

However, the real reasons for our problems proved to be our failure to respect clients and to communicate honourably and completely with employees. My business had poor management and accountability systems and lacked thoughtful and effective business planning.

Learning how to succeed

Now, new rules and processes have changed our business's character and culture.

Everyone communicates through regular meetings and appreciates that we must always respect our clients.

We understand that we will achieve the greatest and most satisfying results by doing what we enjoy, and doing it well. No one here is pushed into a corporate straightjacket. Employees are encouraged to work independently to achieve the greatest personal happiness.

For example, I recently hired an entrepreneurial employee with a side-business. We established rules clearly defining the boundaries between his own business and ours, and built in a joint venture to grow the new business as a separate entity.

In Washington, when we realized the traditional print media would not work, a local business leader suggested we launch an online publication. With that support, we started the *Design and Construction Report*. In the process, we completed the integration of traditional media and powerful new social networking resources. We are still learning how this new multi-faceted media can succeed and are excited by the combination of instantaneous relationship-building, live networking, and the ability to integrate print, audio and visual capacities into a complete marketing package.

How to turn your insights into results

How can you gain from this book's insights?

You may want to work in our organization. If you are interested in becoming a regional construction news publisher, read Appendix B.

You may need to leave the industry. You should, if you are doing the work "just for the money" or "just to survive." Find a way to integrate your vocation with your passions. You might discover your answers in a flash of insight.

Economic circumstances may force you out of your current job and comfort zone. Alternatively, you may simply need to endure a less-than-perfect environment to bring in enough money to live, while you develop your strengths outside of working hours.

Can you start your own business?

If you really enjoy your work but lose your job, consider starting your own business. Enterprises started during recessions are often much more successful than ones established in good times. You need to work hard and effectively to survive and you will develop good work habits that you will find to be exceptionally profitable when conditions improve.

"Yes, but I need to feed my family (or myself), and I'm not ready to take that risk," you might say. Not everyone should run a business. Still, you have choices. If you are working, do your very best and pitch in with business development and marketing support. Your boss is not going to fire you if you bring in sales. If you are unemployed, volunteer. Help others and you will help yourself.

You are not alone

If you own your own business and see the writing on the wall because of the economic circumstances, you can find solace in knowing you are not alone. This problem is not your making. You can survive.

Consult with professional advisers. Your best advice may be close to home, within your trade associations or groups. You will need to be open, humble, and practical. Whatever you do, work hard to preserve and develop your brand. Maintain positive relationships with current and potential (including former) clients.

Follow through on opportunities and initiatives. Your employees may have good suggestions. Listen.

Be yourself

Have fun. Be yourself. Respect others (especially your employees and clients). Understand that the most important key to construction (or any) marketing success is your ability to do your work so well, with so much passion, that you truly are among the top 20 per cent in your field.

With these strengths and similar attitudes among your employees and supporters, do you think a little (or, for that matter, a big) recession will thwart your growth and progress? I think not.

You can – and certainly will – succeed when you realize the magic formula for construction marketing success is to do what you love doing and to share your passions with the people around you.

Appendix A

Construction marketing resources

The Construction Marketing Ideas blog and constructionmarketingideas.com

For additional resources, *Construction Marketing Ideas* is the best place for you to start. The blog/web site provides direct links to associations, other relevant sites, and resources, and of course you can check for current developments and use the search function for background research.

The *Construction Marketing Ideas* newsletter

Published every other week, this newsletter provides current insights and provides you an opportunity to have your individual questions answered. You can register online at the *Construction Marketing Ideas* site.

The Society for Marketing Professional Services (SMPS)

Visit SMPS (www.smps.org) for information about this vitally important national association dedicated to architectural, engineering and construction marketing. SMPS has local chapters in most major U.S. cities, as well as Toronto, Canada. In addition to networking, special chapter and online programs, as well as a comprehensive bookstore, the association has archived significant and useful resources for members. (SMPS, while open to everyone, focuses more on the government, business-to-business and institutional markets.)

Useful websites and discussion forums

In addition to internal listserves within SMPS, I have found value in these sites:

Contractortalk.com and **Remodelcrazy.com**

Both sites have forums dedicated to the construction industry, with an emphasis on the residential/consumer markets. Remodel Crazy not surprisingly, focuses on remodelling. Contractor Talk, however, has specialized groups representing the major sub trades.

Other associations

I believe that association membership and participation are among the most effective marketing methods, especially for business-to-business marketing, but perhaps are among the most under-utilized resources in the consumer marketplace. Of course, the challenge is in determining which associations to join. Review your current clients' interests and see which ones match your own values.

Other blogs and websites

You'll find a comprehensive listing of blogs and relevant sites at *Construction Marketing Ideas* website.

Appendix "B"

Social Networking:
A rapidly evolving environment

In the weeks before this book went to press, the Social Networking phenomena reached a new and exciting stage. Sites such as Facebook, Twitter, and LinkedIn have moved to the forefront with new innovations, creating intriguing marketing opportunities and challenges in a rapidly changing environment.

The single most powerful element of the social networking sites is their ability to create immediate and wide-ranging personal relationships between you, your colleagues and your current and potential clients. They can build, or destroy, your reputation in a moment.

The key to success in this evolving environment is to connect with your readers/community and be authentic. You need to be prepared for intensive two-way communication (and much talk about your business that you cannot control directly).

The advice here reflects my understanding of the state-of-the art of social networking in February, 2010. If you are reading an older edition of this book, you should check online at Construction Marketing Ideas for current thoughts as the story is changing.

I've noted elsewhere in this book how we built the online *Design and Construction Report* (dcnreport.com) from relationships developed through the Design and Construction Network (www.mydcn.com.) This group, founded by Tim Klabunde in the Washington, D.C. area in early 2009, is one of the first successful applications of the LinkedIn "groups" system, and now has more than 4,000 members.

In December, 2009, I decided to set up my own group, aptly named the Construction Marketing Ideas group. I sent out several thousand automated invitations through the LinkedIn system, and within a few weeks, the group had more than 400 members. It is growing at between 20 and 30 members a week.

The group has inspired discussions, enhanced connections, and of course, assisted in building my own reputation and brand.

You may find you can set up your own business or industry-related group and make further connections with it. Alternatively, you can join and participate in groups relevant to your interests.

Recently, I discovered Facebook has also set up a similar "groups" function. This reflects the competitive dynamics of the online space and may prove to be a useful resource in the future.

Facebook has evolved from a college and young person's social networking site to a powerful business resource, with the system's allowance for businesses to set up special "fan pages," which allow companies and organizations to create their own site, and invite Facebook users to sign on as supporters or fans.

The difference between a regular Facebook account and a business page is that you cannot access all the personal information you would of real friends, but you can gather up to 5,000 fans on your site, and build a virtual community of true supporters.

This service is free, and you will want to explore how other businesses or organizations use it. You can search "Construction Marketing Ideas" on Facebook or, if you would like to see a truly successful fan page in operation, visit Tim Nagle's Remodel Buddy site.

Twitter

Despite the fact that our company employs one of the earliest Twitter users, Daniel Smith, (we discovered him through an equally early LinkedIn job listing), we have found limited direct application of Twitter to our business yet, except to support and supplement other online initiatives. However, with a variety of automated resources, you may find Twitter effectively enhances your network and can provoke immediate responses.

Blogging

I discuss blogging extensively in Chapter 8. In my case, the *Construction Marketing Ideas* blog is the glue that binds the various social networking initiatives and resources together, but you may find it is a secondary resource as you explore and develop these areas.

Advertising on social networking sites

You may wish to experiment with advertising on Facebook and LinkedIn. Some advertisers have reported impressive results. However, the space is so new that it is hard to draw conclusions or give recommendations. I think you should dip your fingers into the advertising water carefully.

Social networking and the search engines

Undoubtedly Google and other search engines "like" effective social networking sites, and Google is creating an interface that will allow you to connect your social networking activities with your search – it is still an experiment as I write this book.

Controlling your environment

Social networking sites represent word-of-mouth in hyper-drive. If you mistreat a client or create a bad experience, your name can be mud, instantly. People will respect the opinions of their friends within the social networking groups, and the bad news can spread virally throughout the Internet.

Your best way to overcome this potential problem is to be proactive. Obviously you should ensure your client experience standards are impeccable. As well, if you are authentic, communicate openly and respectfully, and don't play tricks on your audience, you will be able to deflect criticisms as your fans will rally to your support against detractors. However, if you are late to the game, your reputation may be permanently damaged before you even know the problem has occurred.

An evolving story

I've written this chapter as an Appendix just before putting the book to press, because it could only be written now and it will likely need to be revised in the months ahead. Fortunately, changes can be made quickly and you will hear about them on the blog and our social networking pages. As well, you can request updates by communicating with me at buckshon@cnrgp.com.

Appendix C

Working with the Construction News and Report Group of Companies

Regional Construction industry publications

The Construction News and Report Group of Companies grew from a regional construction newspaper serving Ottawa, Canada, *Ottawa Construction News*, which started publication in 1989-90 and is published monthly now. At the time (and still at present), some local associations published journals, but few independent regional construction industry publications existed.

We expanded the business to serve the Greater Toronto Area (*GTA Construction Report*) and developed a publication included as a supplement to the regional publications that serves all of Ontario (*Ontario Construction Report*).

In 2000, the business expanded to the U.S. Currently, we publish *Triangle/Triad Construction News* and *Charlotte Construction News*, serving these major North Carolina markets.

The Design and Construction Report (dcnreport.com)

Our flagship U.S. publication, *Washington Construction News* (serving the metropolitan Washington, D.C. area), has evolved into a combination print/online magazine associated with the Design and Construction Network (mydcn.com), which is headquartered in Northern Virginia, but has subgroups throughout the U.S. and Canada.

Publicity opportunities and resources

Our publications earn most of their revenue from advertising, largely in supplier-supported editorial profiles that cost the profiled business little if any money. This form of supply-chain marketing is common in the publishing business; we seek to deliver value far beyond the scope of the conventional "support your client" advertising. In fact the *Construction Marketing Ideas* blog and this book trace their roots to initiatives to provide enhanced service to advertising clients.

You can receive a free e-book, *The Art and Science of Publicity*, by emailing publicity@cnrgp.com or visiting the relevant page on the Construction Marketing Ideas site.

Speaking and consulting

CNRG President Mark Buckshon co-ordinates webinars and presentations and is available for speaking engagements. He also can provide individualized marketing consulting or recommend consultants who may be better suited to your business. For more information, call Mark at 888-432-3555 ext 224 or email buckshon@cnrgp.com.

Working with the CNRGP as an employee or contractor

We encourage you to communicate with us if you are interested in becoming an associate regional publisher or would like to help develop new market possibilities. Work can be co-ordinated on an employee/employer, independent contractor or joint venture basis, depending on its potential and what makes the most sense for everyone. For more information email Chase at chase@cnrgp.com.

Your questions and inquires

Please feel free to visit the Construction Marketing Ideas site and let us know your thoughts.

Index

8424

CPSIA information can be obtained at www.ICGtesting.com
Printed in the USA
LVOW131614200412

278498LV00005B/123/P